DAYS OF OUR LIVES LIE IN FRAGMENTS

OTHER BOOKS BY GEORGE GARRETT

FICTION

King of the Mountain
The Finished Man
Which Ones Are the Enemy?
In the Briar Patch
Cold Ground Was My Bed Last Night
Do, Lord, Remember Me
A Wreath for Garibaldi
Death of the Fox
The Magic Striptease
The Succession
An Evening Performance
Poison Pen
Entered from the Sun
The Old Army Game
The King of Babylon Shall Not Come Against You

POETRY

The Reverend Ghost: Poems
The Sleeping Gypsy and Other Poems
Abraham's Knife and Other Poems
For a Bitter Season: New and Selected Poems
Welcome to the Medicine Show
Luck's Shining Child
The Collected Poems of George Garrett

PLAYS

Sir Slob and the Princess
Enchanted Ground

NONFICTION

James Jones
Understanding Mary Lee Settle
The Sorrows of Fat City
Whistling in the Dark
My Silk Purse and Yours

For Michael
All love
G

DAYS OF

OUR LIVES

LIE IN

FRAGMENTS

GEORGE GARRETT

New and Old Poems
1957–1997

LOUISIANA STATE UNIVERSITY PRESS
Baton Rouge
1998

Designer: Melanie O'Quinn Samaha
Typeface: 10 point Sabon
Typesetter: G&S Typesetters, Inc.
Printer and binder: Thomson-Shore, Inc.

Library of Congress Cataloging-in-Publication Data

Garrett, George P., 1929–
    Days of our lives lie in fragments : new and old poems, 1957–1997
/ George Garrett.
        p.   cm.
    ISBN 0-8071-2283-1 (alk. paper). — ISBN 0-8071-2284-X (pbk. : alk. paper)
    I. Title
PS3557.A72D39   1998
811'.54—dc21   97-42577
                                                                                              CIP

Most of the poems herein have been selected from: *The Reverend Ghost* (Scribner's, 1957), copyright © 1956, 1957 by George Garrett; *The Sleeping Gypsy and Other Poems* (University of Texas Press, 1958), copyright © 1958 by the University of Texas Press; *Abraham's Knife and Other Poems* (University of North Carolina Press, 1961), copyright © 1958, 1959, 1960, 1961 by George Garrett; *For a Bitter Season: New and Selected Poems* (University of Missouri Press, 1967), copyright © 1956, 1957, 1958, 1959, 1960, 1961, 1962, 1963, 1964, 1965, 1966, 1967 by George Garrett; *Welcome to the Medicine Show* (Palaemon Press, 1978), copyright © 1978 by George Garrett; *Luck's Shining Child* (Palaemon Press, 1981), copyright © 1981 by George Garrett; and *The Collected Poems of George Garrett* (University of Arkansas Press, 1984), copyright © 1956, 1957, 1958, 1959, 1960, 1961, 1962, 1963, 1964, 1965, 1966, 1967, 1978, 1981, 1984 by George Garrett.

    Grateful acknowledgment is also made to the editors of the following periodicals, in which some of the poems, or versions of them, first appeared: *Approach, Artemus, Blue Buildings, Cargoes, Carolina Quarterly, Chronicles, Coastlines, College English, Compass Review, Contempora, Epos, Francis Marion Review, Harvest, Hemispheres, Hollins Critic, Janus, Kudzu, Latitudes, Lycoming Review, Mademoiselle, Michigan Quarterly Review, Mill Mountain Review, Plume & Sword, Poetry Northwest, Prairie Schooner, Princeton Alumni Weekly, Princeton University Library Chronicle, Rapier, Review La Booche, Sewanee Review, Three Rivers Poetry Journal, Transatlantic Review, Vanderbilt Poetry Review,* and *Willow Springs.*

    "The Long and Short of It" originally appeared in *A New Geography of Poets,* edited by Edward Field and Gerald Locklin (University of Arkansas Press, 1992). "Envy" originally appeared in *The Peregrine Reader,* edited by Mikel Vause and Carl Porter (Gibbs Smith, 1997). "Dead of Winter" originally appeared in a flyer entitled *Spring Poetry Festival: Salvatore Quasimodo* (1960).

The paper in this book meets the guidelines for permanence and durability of the Committee on Production Guidelines for Book Longevity of the Council on Library Resources. ∞

Rightly is the sea compared to this world, for it is sometimes serene and pleasant to navigate on, sometimes also very rough and terrible to be on. So is this world; sometimes it is desirable and pleasant to dwell in, sometimes also it is very rugged and mingled with divers things, so that it is too often very unpleasant to inhabit. Sometimes we are hale, sometimes sick; now joyful, and again in great affliction; therefore is this life, as we before said, compared to the sea.

—Aelfric, Abbot of Eynsham
"Homily for Mid-Lent Sunday"

This book is gratefully dedicated to the memory of some poets, each of whom was wonderfully kind and generous and encouraging when it mattered greatly: R. P. Blackmur, John Hall Wheelock, Marianne Moore, Babette Deutsch, Louis Coxe, James Dickey, May Sarton, Bink Noll, Paul Ramsey, Richard Elman, O. B. Hardison, Jr., and John Ciardi.

CONTENTS

I. NEW POEMS

II. OLD POEMS

from *For a Bitter Season* (1967)

I NEW POEMS

Postcard

One of these times very soon
I will have and hold a day
blank as a new pillowcase
or a field of fresh snow.
And then and there once again
I will lay down my head, I will
make angels in the wet snow.
I will write words words words,
as you do, and will sign my name,
naming my new poems like children,
calling them home from the dark.

Days of Our Lives Lie in Fragments

In memory of O. B. Hardison, Jr.

A calm clear morning on the York River
that we have both known and sailed together,
a calm day and cool with the first touch

of autumn abroad, with geese at dawn
flying high and south in ragged formations
over the rocky shoreline lit by a rising sun.

Hours later in my boathouse, alone,
thinking about you and your sudden death,
I listen to a grayback gull perched on a piling,

cry out sounds that surely must be
an entirely incongruous laughter.
Tide turning; days of our lives lie in fragments.

There's no plot here, no narrative to follow,
a cold familiar voice whispers in my ear. I have
no reply, though I hope for something different, better.

Think how they slip away one at a time,
out of the light of all our ambiguous loves
and into the blaze and bright of another weather.

And soon, soon enough, we shall all cross over
out of these shadowy seasons of sooner and later,
each alone as can be with pain and sorrow.

See how, splendid as geese in flight,
they now join hands to move in a dance
to a music we cannot hear, can only guess at.

And I think I can see you there among the dancers
and I suddenly guess the music is the laughter
of angels, citizens of incredible ever-after.

Something wakes me, makes me step to the window:
tide running out, the river on fire with the sunset
and gulls overhead, white wings riding the wind.

Not many now remember,
fewer and fewer remember,
most because they never knew
in the first place, being lucky
and too young, and others
because they are too few and too old
already; but, anyway, I remember

the three reasons most often advanced
in those innocent days before the War
as strong and self-evident argument
that Adolf Hitler was crazy:
First, that he was a strict vegetarian.
Second, that he did not smoke or permit
any smoking around him, being convinced

that smoking cigarettes was somehow
linked to lung cancer.
Third, because he went around saying
that the Volkswagen, laughable beetle,
was the car of the future.

Maybe God, in all his power and majesty,
can still enjoy the irony of it.

Miles later, young man, old soldier, I
stand at the bar of a *gasthaus*

in Leonding, a country village near Linz,
lean against the dark, smooth, polished wood,
drinking and listening to very old men
remember the days of the Austro-Hungarian Empire.
Happens that Hitler's father lived here then.

And they can remember him and his son, too,
who every evening came to this *gasthaus*

for a bucket of beer for his father's supper.
Would stand there patiently waiting where
you are standing now, then, pail in hand,
set off under the early stars along a lane
towards the lights of home, whistling in the dark.

Everyone who knew agrees that then and later
he was a wonderful whistler, worth listening to.
I lean back against the bar to picture
how he was then, lips puckered,
whistling tunes I do not know,
beer rich and foamy, sloshing in the pail,
smell of woodsmoke, cooking meat and cabbage.

And, invisible and implacable, always
the wide smile of God upon His creatures, one and all,
great and small, among them this little pale-faced boy,
for whom He has arranged some enormous surprises,
beyond any kind of imagining, even myself,
drunk in this place, years from home, imagining it.

Inch by Inch

In memory of John Ciardi

Even as, inch by living inch,
I contrive to chip and cut and carve
myself into various and sundry parts—

first, of course, the fingers
and the toes, then ears and nose,
these offered, as it were, in the words

of *The Book of Common Prayer,* to be
"a reasonable, holy and living sacrifice."
Eyes before sex, arms before legs;

next the thin peeled skin and last
the bloody mess of muscles and meat,
fat and lonely internal organs . . .

Must we be universal donors, John?

Much too much to hope for.
Better (and you knew it and said so,
so well and so many times)

to spend our skin and bones, to pay
out blood and breath upon
a wholly unimportant poem,

something reasonably simple and simply
(while memory still burns) unforgettable:
you and I, one time, late on my front porch

in York Harbor, Maine, drinking
stone fences—your special favorite
apple jack and apple cider, all

the fumes and essences of Eden;
two old guys feeling no pain
underneath the brightly reeling stars,

while nearby, shiny and smooth
as a blacksnake, the river is rising
to high tide, inch by living inch.

Figure of Speech

It's a doggie dog world.
—student paper

For years my litter of wounds
moved quietly, obedient and gentle,
well-trained, eager to please.
Loved my quick heels and the tight leash,
begged cutely, fetched and rolled over,
and licked the fingers that fed them.

Now they return, a gaunt and feral pack,
each and every one presenting
a noisy mouth, rich with cruel teeth
and drooling tongue. See their red eyes,
how the hair stands up as they turn against
each other, killing for my choicest parts.

Something to see,
something really to behold:
how, sudden and graceful,
that redwing blackbird
can and does now light
on the tip of a cattail
and can ride with it,
rock and roll with it,
then steady (tick and tock)
keep time in empty air.

First Bluejay

Rain beading on buds of dogwood,
glistening, too, on first thrust
of daffodils and crocus
like the shine of light on bayonets;
and here he comes now, the early
courtier of light and air, big boy
strutting his colors of blue and white,
daring the sky to cast off its gray cloak,
betting the trees will raise their hands
again in green and bright surrender.

Lord, but I do dearly love
these, your large, slow reedy messengers,
your spies clad in shiny feathers,
sentinels of high places squawking
and cawing arrivals and departures,
raggedy fliers rising in a black caucus
or, grounded, the shifty epitome
of pure swagger and bravado.
Old crows, noisy flock,
we came through bad weather together
when all the trees were a cruel glitter
of ice and earth was a hard-hearted stranger
who wished only catastrophe upon us,
you and I, shabby and insufferably proud,
perched here to witness the robins' return.

(a letter to Brendan Galvin)

Over Peter Taylor's
brand new and expensive
toothpick fence,
through the glossy green
shine of my magnolia leaves,
directly into the back yard,
it could have been the ghost
of Ted Roethke or Big Jim
Dickey in a Halloween costume
or maybe even ole Galway Kinnell
cultivating his familiar image,
but was in fact a black
bear cub standing about six-four
and coming in at close to
three hundred pounds.
Quick and agile,
he was a real one like
one of yours, Brendan,
poet of the real and true,
his bristles stiff as a toilet brush
and a strong scent to raise hair
on the neck and back
of my black and tan hound
barking safely in the house.
Bear took one look at me
and the old cop and the young
Ranger with his tranquilizer gun,
then turned and went,
light as Baryshnikov,
over my ragged back hedge,
down the dry creek bed and,
quicker than I ever saw
anything larger than a squirrel
move, vanished into a shimmer
of leaves and afternoon light.
Forever as far as I was concerned.
Cop and Ranger lost him, too,
on the other side of Route 29

in a patch of pine woods near
the football practice field.
And that's about the size,
the long and short of it.
I don't know what it means,
Brendan, except that maybe
even an ordinary back yard
can yield up a share of
surprises. Meantime it gives
me plenty to think about.
I picture the bear, unnoticed,
joining in at football practice,
making the team, going to classes,
and on Saturday playing defense
against Virginia Tech,
first big game we won.
I picture a Tech player
complaining to his coach:
"Hey, coach, that guy
across from me, he's the ugliest
dude I've ever seen.
Got hair all over, head to toe,
red eyes and something like claws,
too; and I'm not going back
out there without a gun."

Not only the pleasures of dust,
of dry, stained pages and the out-of-date
card that proves nobody has even checked
this one out in a decade and not more
than half a dozen times in my whole lifetime.
       GENE DERWOOD . . . LLOYD FRANKENBERG . . .
ALFRED HAYES . . . COMAN LEAVENWORTH . . . JOHN
THOMPSON, JR. . . . .

But also all of these names and so many
more, not really forgotten, but not to be found,
either, anywhere else but here in the stacks
on shelves where Robinson's darkest inches
preserve the anonymous dignity of the unfamous.
       MARYA ZATURENSKA . . . CALE YOUNG RICE . . .
H. PHELPS PUTNAM . . . WILLIAM ELLERY LEONARD . . .
ALFRED KREYMBORG . . .

And one great secret is simply this—how, taken
together, cheek-by-jowl, these people, these poets,
are often so much alike in form and substance
and more democratic in excellence and virtue
than anyone might have otherwise imagined.
       MADELINE GLEASON . . . ROBERT HORAN . . .
MYRON O'HIGGINS . . . BYRON VAZAKAS . . .

Years ago in the Village at the Sam Remo
I bought poems from Maxwell Bodenheim
at fifty cents a pop. Once at the Museum
of Modern Art I watched W. H. Auden unsuccessfully
try to check a bottle of champagne like a coat.
       HELEN ADAM . . . EBBE BORREGAARD . . .
ADAM DRINAN . . . MURRAY NOSS . . . ELDER OLSON . . .

But what of all the unfamous others, ourselves
I mean, still alive and on fire and in love
with the taste of words and the making of poems?
Who will come here afterwards to blow the dust away
and disturb the peace and oblivion we have earned?

    FRED CHAPPELL . . . KELLY CHERRY . . . R. H. W.
DILLARD . . . BRENDAN GALVIN . . . GEORGE GARRETT . . .
DAVID SLAVITT . . . HENRY TAYLOR . . .

In this fat book I find
a signature, my own, my name
done in my same hand, but different.
I could not make it that way now.

Summer of 1947 it would have to be.
The copyright is dated 1946—
A Little Treasury of Modern Poetry:
The Best Poems of the 20th Century.

A bit early then, wouldn't you say?,
with this bloody century not yet half done,
to be collecting and publishing the best.
Not at that time when everything was new

and wonderful, when so many of these poets,
words on pages, their pictures in the back,
were new names to me and even now
look younger than any of us ever were.

Day Lewis, Eberhart, George Barker
and John Manifold are purely and simply
smiling and now are sure enough dead
or dying. The others look deadly serious.

And all but a precious few of them
are long gone to glory or oblivion.
Does anyone alive still miss Gene Derwood
with those wild eyes and that funny hat?

Does anybody else but myself and Mary Lee
Settle still march to Manifold's "Fife Tune"?
Is anyone around to rejoice at the rhymes
of Hildegarde Flanner's "Noon on Alameda Street"?

The child who believed he was a man
and scribbled my name in the flyleaf here
went forth like Ransom's "Captain Carpenter"
to read his way through the book of wounds.

And this book sitting on its dark shelf
for years, a buried treasure of shining words,
a safe house assigned to all the dead poets
he loved and cherished at first sight.

Who are these privateers who tack and trim,
guided by their ambition and their whim?
—Jean De Sponde, *Sonnets on Death* IX
(tr. David Slavitt)

Oh I could name
a dozen poets I'd like to send a ton
of rotted sheep manure to, if I could be sure
of delivery at quarter of four in the morning.
—Virgil, *Eclogues* III (Palaemon)
(tr. David Slavitt)

1. DUMBO

That Menalcus
has really and truly
read and fully comprehended
the gnarled and knotty
(not to mention Nazi)
words and works
of Martin Heidegger,
I find about as likely
as that one fine day
all the elephants of Ringling
Brothers, Barnum and Bailey
will flap their huge gray ears
and fly away in fabulous formation.

If that ever happens, Menalcus,
don't be caught
standing underneath.

2. HORROR SHOW

Picture ole Palaemon,
his baseball cap backwards
on his handsome head,
driving his dusty pickup
to park at a drive-in theater
and see a horror movie—

Frankenstein Meets the Space Monster.
Tight close shot of his habitual
serious expression with its post-
Vendlerian tilt of earned and honest
pride, now slightly wrinkled,
more baffled than amused.
This movie (he is thinking)
is it like a joke or what?
One of these days I guess
I'm going to have to learn
a couple of jokes and maybe
do a little homework
on my sense of humor.

3. THE GIFT

All the bright and shiny
scissors of a certain village
in Croatia are marching, marching.

Scissors are marching proudly,
followed by thimbles, needles and thread
directly to Durham, New Hampshire.

Meanwhile in the windy and treeless
Highlands of faraway Scotland
a significant number of sheep

have offered up their fleece to make
the wool which very soon these tools
will make into something wonderful.

It will become a suit,
a sturdy and elegant tweed suit,
especially made for Alexis.

The fabric, like its source,
is docile and cooperative;
but (alas) not all the tailors

of Yugoslavia have taught
obedience to the scissors and needles.
These things will quarrel, and the suit

will turn out to be very strange.
To wear it at all, Alexis
will have to drag his right leg

as if it were wooden and longer
than the other one. Will have to shrug
his right shoulder and twist his left arm

behind his back. "Look at that poor man,"
a New Hampshire woman will whisper.
"But, ah!, what a beautiful suit."

4. BELT BUCKLE

It's not
        the celebrated dark glasses
nor the elegant cashmere blazer
        nor those pale designer jeans
nor even the colorful Brooks Brothers
        shirts asserted by
(this season) the thinnest shoelace of
        a necktie that I've seen so far
and not even the running shoes or sometimes,
more formal, classic penny loafers.

None of the above things
        so much as the huge and shiny
silver and turquoise
        Navajo belt buckle
(worth about the price of my Chevette,
        I reckon)
which I summon up whenever I consider
the letter and the spirit of Corydon.
        It isn't exactly like Achilles' shield

in Homer or Auden either;
　　　　but whenever you look
in that buckle you can see how truly small you are
　　　　and how small everybody else is, too,
and everything except the wide sky and the lazy
　　　　clouds (white or black no matter).
It's a space, the place where it is possible
　　　　to imagine, as Corydon says he does,
the amazing marriage of Emily and Walt.

5. PUNCH LINE

All of a sudden
people are telling
Meliboeus jokes
in New York City.
His own great line
("Lunch with Harry
at Lutece") isn't
all that funny any more.
Anyway, here's one
that I overheard:
Cab pulls up in front
of the Plaza and out
steps Meliboeus, in person,
tall and handsome as ever.
Up runs this beautiful
blond groupie and kneels
at his feet as if in prayer.
"Oh, Mr. Meliboeus," she pleads,
"please let me be
your slave for life.
Permit me to cover
you with kisses. Allow
me to devote myself
to the satisfaction of
your every whim and need."
"That's all well and good," says he,
"but what's in it for me?"

6. PARTIAL REVISION FOR D.H.

(If the shoe fits . . .)

Since, despite my prayers and best wishes,
you are evidently still alive and well,
manners require that I hereby offer
apology for my premature epitaph,
though not for its heartfelt injunction
to go straight and directly to hell.

7. MOI AUSSI

To be fair
I must report
the skinny on myself.

Seated upon the john
like Lyndon and Luther,
I am inspired.
I am suddenly able
to define literary failure.
It's when you know
death will do nothing
to enhance or advance you,
when even suicide would not be
a good career move.

ENVY

Calls itself injustice.
Calls itself the grim, appropriate answer
to a swarm of bitter questions.
Lies heavy, heavy on my heart.

Names me fool at first sight.
Makes me fool of the feast of the dead.
Serves me ditch water and mouldy bread.
Winks at me with your green eyes.

PRIDE

What I have done
(no thanks to you and you and you),
what I have earned
by fire and blood and iron,
I'll share with you now in silver and gold.
Come closer and kiss my scars.
Kneel down to lick the dust from my shoes.

SLOTH

A great soft beast
has swallowed my body whole
and I rest easy here,
hearing nothing more
than the sonorous music
of his mighty snores.

Or this: a woman the size
of a snow-capped mountain
allows me to doze in the shade
of her breasts, permits me
the dream of floating free
in the dead sea between her thighs.

I would gladly write you a poem
about all this (and more as well)
if my lazy words would not
drown like ink on a blotter,
if my story were strong enough
to shatter your dream like a bell.

LUST
It happens
comes to pass
like it or not
quick as the flame
of a struck match
in a dark room

Not purely and simply
maybe not at all
a matter of meat
breasts flank and rump
conspiring to promise
everything and nothing

but something else
more slight and subtle
sunlight on hair
clean line of calf
hands like pale wings
her voice like birdsong

And I again
hear voices and fumble
to strike the match of myself
in the darkest part of myself
to light my candle
and let it burn

GREED

To possess
To take and to own
to have and to hold
if only by naming
every part and parcel
bag and baggage
every living thing
if only by leaving
my name everywhere
my ineradicable initials
my fingerprints in bronze
To settle for nothing
less than sky writing
(behold how bold
against the shine
of royal white and blue)
I take possession of the here and now
and everything is mine mine mine

GLUTTONY

Charles Laughton as Henry VIII
chomping down on a chicken leg
like a world-class cannibal chef
presenting a well-cooked missionary.
(*Yum! Yum! Divinity!*)

King of toads and toadstools,
I am a Rumplestiltskin who
consumes whatever grows or walks
or swims, turning it into excrement,
calling it gourmet peanut butter.

Fill me with groans like a bagpipe.
Stuff me and swell me like
a slaphappy hot-air balloon.
In hell let the children of Saturn
play my clean bones like piano keys.

WRATH

Picture God in blackface,
rolling His infinite eyes,
grinning a mouthful of white stars,
doing jumpdown, slamdunk, hiphop
to the tune of angelic banjos
while all of our cries and curses
fall lightly on deaf ears.

Years ago I wrote a poem
seething with anger, ending:
"Let God forgive me. Isn't
forgiveness His stock-in-trade?"
But, God Almighty, wasn't I dead
wrong? Anything good like that
fixing to happen, it's up to us.

Which means it won't.
Which means while all the company
of heaven be singing and dancing,
shucking and jiving and talking
angelic ebonics, we'll still be biting
our bloody tongues to pieces,
breaking each other's bones in two.

AMBITION

I will think anything.
I will gladly believe everything.
I will do anything,
anything at all,
to win the love and praise
of perfect strangers.

I will worship both
your going out and your coming in.
I will erase myself like a misspelled word.
I will dazzle you with sleights

of hand. And if and when
you finally and fully reward me,
I will offer the contempt you so richly deserve.

SELF-PITY

> I suffer from low self of steam.
> —student paper

You are too late.
Altogether impossible now
to heal my old wounds,
to satisfy my wealth
of grievances, to solace
the widows and orphans who
squat in the home of my heart.

It is my latest pleasure
to laugh into the face
of your sad concern for me.
It's a teeth-grinding joy
to shrug away your touch,
to grit those selfsame teeth
and wish you nothing but well.

In the absence of justice
I make up my own.

In the absence of equity
I stand upon privilege.

Tempted by abstract despair
I herewith deny the Holy Ghost.

Rejecting the purity of reason
I savor my own mindless fevers.

On the blank face of virtue
I celebrate antique vices.

In full view of humility I scorn
everything that is not already praised.

In response to your gift of love
I will gladly steal you blind.

What is it will free me
from the bitter taste
of myself?

Is there a stranger
whose kiss is sweet enough
to do the job?

Is there a liquor
from amber waves of grain
distilled and cooled

that can fool me
for a rich and smoky time
of satisfaction?

Is there an ancient prayer
long gone and forgotten
which can return

in the rush of memory
to light and enlighten me
the whole way home?

God Save the King

Foolish old man. More fool
than your own Fool. Father
of monsters . . . all but one
(*and what need one?*).

How many actors
then or now on blasted heath,
in stormy, don't-know-why weather,
have played the long part,
memorized and mouthed the hard
sayings, comically staggered
under the dead weight
of a dead Cordelia?

How many of us have wept
at those words, your ruins,
old father of actors and sorrows,
old fool, foolish old friend?

Dark prince of intellectuals, that broody boy,
dressed all in black and talking to himself out loud
too much, ghosted, driven, finally stone dead on stage
among the others, not counting ole Rosencrantz
and Guildenstern, who are also as dead as dead can be,
which is quite dead enough, and nobody left in charge
but young Fortinbras, who will never pass muster
with the intellectual types who gladly do anything
not to do anything but talk out loud about it,
and, alas, poor Horatio left to do all the talking,
this sad show and tell we love so much, those tales
where, just or not, the great and even the good fall
                                                    down.

Five Card Draw, Jacks Are Wild

Sneak not away, sir:
alas, poor Lucio, my lad,
it's you, after all, who comes
closest to us in this shameless
day and age, you and ole Iago
(among others) who's not
as funny at least in the same
way; and not, for sure,
the wise Duke, in or out
of his disguise, doing
his damndest to balance
justice and mercy by the book,
he for whom all doors spring open
and the chairs (none with whoopee cushions)
are precisely placed, and to whose thoughts
everyone dutifully listens;
not Isabella, either, whose chastity
is quaintly absolute, whose virtue
we would rather not consider;
but you, sir, a sleaze and a scumbag,
scut and scroyle, a hustler
in a hurry, one of us,
cowardly and sly and trouble
from the word go, whose luck
always runs out in the last scene;
but, luckless or no, will shuffle
the cards and deal and cheat
one more time in hope of heaven
on earth and safety from
the fires of hell, betting it all
and losing always everything.
Whipped first, sir,
and hanged after.

Rufus don't rouse. Randy isn't.
Dr. ("Just call me Dick") Richard
says he feels like a flag
on an utterly breezeless day.
Come quickly, cunts and cuties,
and help the old bishop stand tall,
bareheaded and proud
in eternal benediction.

Duplicity

When our Prince is true and good,
he is the dog who guards the flock;
but when he's false he turns into
the wolf who takes us for his food.

(after a Latin epigram by Sir Thomas More)

Someone
maybe a man
most likely a man with a camera

Loves you
loves the look of you
almost as much as yourself

Something
neither male nor female
most likely the camera itself

Abducts
your fearful spirit
captures nostrils and knees

Someone
most likely myself
falls in love with your name

Dead of Winter

Your clear hands call my name.
They dance in the dark light of the fire
With the odor and oakwood and roses
And death. Dead of winter.

What became of the starving birds?
They fell into a waste of snow.
So it is with words.
They flash like sudden angels, go
Away like ghosts. So with the trees
And us, too, made of morning breeze.

(after Salvatore Quasimodo)

Ghosts

Arriving completely unannounced
indeed honestly uninvited,
in dreams of course
but also in a stab
and shock like the sting
of irrepressible memory,

my own dead and wounded
rise up from dark places
to strike me deaf and dumb
as any stone. O fathers
and mothers moving in twilight
stay and be still

as you were and are
in (always) fading memory
pray be smiling, kindly wait,
be easy on us living and scarred
kinfolks who came to love and grief
too little and too late.

David (Again)

Thinking on the dead king, the poet
      and lover, the killer

Who toppled the giant and held up his
      head by the snarled hair

(Just so, you can believe, his own son's head
      of hair entangled him)

Thinking now again how the words came and the
      music to fit them

Thinking how often those words came to flashing life
      like a startled flock

Of wild birds and flew in time to the music
      to hurry them home

How it must have been to be the chosen scribe of
      the Lord our God

Hearing not words or music but something like
      the secret voice of fire

But myself on fire and chiefly thinking
      here and now again

Of the old king old man as old as I am
      and cold cold cold

Warming himself by the soft white heat
      of clear smooth skin

Taking young bodies to bed like a feather
      pillow to clutch and hold

Against which to press his wrinkled face
      and call forth dreams

And finally summoning (again) the darkest dream, of death,
      the giant who will not fall down

Jacob (Again)

Came then in the dark
Out of the dark a dark
Man without name or number
    a brute fact
    a bad dream
labor of love and death

Came then made of dirt
and water at the water's edge
a man thing hairy as a hedge
    a brutal dream
    the bitter fact
breaker of bones and hearts

All alone trickster and thief
liar and lover I came
seeking to find myself
    and met instead
    this being made
wholly of flame and air

How we rolled and wrestled
then in the water and dirt
and breathed together
    all night long
    by the black fire
of a burning bush

Came then when first light
dazzled and blinded the shore
my crippled self now newly named
    and never again to be
    the broken being
that I had been before.

Judith

What I have learned about men
besides the astonishing amount of blood
that rages along the dark highways and byways
of their hairy, hungry bodies.
(I had not thought of that
nor thought the old man would offer up
such a rush and rain of blood
such spurts and clots and gouts.)
Besides that, then, and the news to me
that pain, mine, can be and was his pleasure
and that this man, his voice trained
and suited to the habits of high command,
would plead with me like a child,
would beg me not to cease and desist
the gift of my suffering, his joy.
Besides all that I learned another thing—
how they all want to die then and there
in the groaning midst of sweaty coupling
to separate themselves from the self
and once and for all to pour out
everything, to become wholly nothing
ever after, to be left empty
as a lost and forgotten glove.
Lord, I did what was right,
what You wanted me to, what he
wanted me to do and be.
then why, tell me why, am I so
lighthearted, why does my light heart
rejoice in itself like a dancing girl?

Riding the Crescent for the first time
since 1966, letting it happen all over again
between Tuscaloosa and Charlottesville,
the old South running directly outside the window,
hugging the tracks, tarpaper shacks and trailers,
a rusty Chevrolet pickup on concrete blocks, a black
boy on a three-speed bike making wild wheelies
in the parking lot of the Mt. Hebron Baptist Church,
piles of the corpses of dead machines
and one whole field of abandoned refrigerators
white as tombstones. Back here kudzu rules the world.

Those singing trains of Faulkner and Thomas Wolfe
are long gone now with all their huffing and puffing
(and my child-self with a cinder in his weepy eye).
We can't any longer look up at the slow curve
and see our steam engine dragging us behind it.
O dark green curtains, upper and lower, of Pullman cars
and a lazy look out the window at the stereotypical
man straddling a mule, himself barefooted
in bib overalls, a straw hat, patiently waiting
for our train to pass by his life and times.
We have all seen him there or remember it that way.
Likewise the white impeccable tablecloth and napkins,
the heavy silverware of the dining car
whose elegant dark waiters roll with the rolling train,
carrying their trays (as Wilbur put it) "tipfingered."

This new train is asking for at least a casual line,
if not exactly for "longer-lined capacious forms."
And I hereby solemnly promise that the solemn name
of Heidegger will not appear in person in poem or train,
Heidegger or Kierkegaard, either, who was never once,
whatever else, on the Crescent from Tuscaloosa
up through blue mountains to Charlottesville
or woke up on a sleeping porch in central Florida
to listen to freight trains whistle and pass by
like carloads of mythical sirens and Rhinemaidens,
calling his name, promising almost everything.

(The Latest Version)

Founding Father (not King no never) George with all
those crude wooden teeth, not smiling often; Thomas Jefferson,

With giddy quill pen, gadgets, and a little mountain;
manic depressive Lincoln (and liberty too), to use an anachronistic

Goldwynism, all "blood and thirsty" and Jefferson
Davis in chains as later Nixon ought to have been, might have
     been too;

Teddy the Sisyphus of San Juan Hill (not Bunker)
and Franklin D., King of the Mountain, not charging up any hill,

Anywhere; LBJ holding court on the john and JFK,
bad back and all, back in the saddle again and again; and now

(Though Grant's the sad face on a fifty) a spoiled country boy
with bad temper and unquenchable appetites, "not tough but
     ruthless,"

Says a friend of this King of Hot Air; And I ask you:
was the man behind the curtain, any of the above, ever truly a wizard?

What has happened, my friends, is this:
we are saying the same things over and over again
because we have to, because there is no other choice.

We are singing the old songs, whistling the same tunes,
each like a small boy in the dark, in a graveyard,
maybe, whistling to reassure the rotten dead

that he, of course, is careless, indifferent, fearless.
We are saying the same things in exactly the same tone of voice
because we have to, because there is no other choice,

except, perhaps, that purity of absolute silence
to which our noisy music does aspire,
with which our music will be well rewarded

all in due time. Meantime, my friends, we must
say again and over again the same few things
(wise or foolish no matter, beauty of bounden duty)

without which the world goes wild and the silent dead
rise up to rattle us daft with their dancing bones
because they have to, because there is no other choice.

Hail to the Chief

(a birthday poem for John Ciardi)

Now comes the time of the tall chief,
the one with the deep voice
like the smoke of dry oak burning,
the one who can shake a spear
in the frightened faces of our enemies
(O silly thanes, O geese,
decked out in silks and satins,
each alone presuming to be a swan);
he who can lay down a serpentine curse
as neat and solid as Jefferson's brick wall;
he who can make a fist
pound like a ten pound maul;
the one who can open his eloquent palms
in a gesture as simple and gentle
as a tulip unfolding toward light;
he who can stand tall and be still
in the darkness close by the campfire's flame
while all our tribe calls out his honored name.

Rag, tag and bobtail.
Button holes without buttons.
Cracked shoes without laces,
with holes in their soles
and rundown heels.

Let your light so shine before men

Scabs and scars and tattoos.
Redrimmed eyes and broken teeth.
Swollen joints and knuckles.
Ingrown toenails and the stink
and itch of private places.

that they may see your good works

Keys to no lock I know of.
Intimate letters from total strangers.
Phone calls with only heavy breathing.
Late knocking and no one is there.
Familiar voices speaking in tongues.

and glorify your Father which is in heaven

Out there on the rainswept field
someone made wholly of rags and tatters
(maybe a scarecrow or a madman)
is turning, turning in the wind
dancing his prayer of praise.

Amen.

II OLD POEMS

The truth of prophets' words, time proves at last—
then poets lie and reinvent the past.

    —a Latin epigram by John Owen
      (translated by David R. Slavitt)

From

The Reverend Ghost

(1957)

Value Judgment

Do not betray me by your smile.
Not with handshake handcuff me,
nor kiss when you should curse, nor be
kind and kill when cure is cruel.

Least of friends are most who grin.
Most of enemies can't grip
so fatally as whose eyes strip
a whole dimension from a man.

The bright queen of the playing card,
the jack of hearts who'll give a wink
to anyone, are true, I think,
more than flesh that's less than kind.

Who calls me zero, I insist
than enemy is nameless worse.
Who'll bless my name with open curse,
I will salute his sacred dust.

A Bargain

Some by trial of fire have failed,
and some in water swallowed whole,
and some have tried to bed on nails
and some on tightrope taken stroll.

Some from parachute have seen
the earth ascending. Some alone,
from cannon fired, have been
brief wonders, and from stone

a few have broken bread.
This one dodges the cruel horns,
that one falls upon the thorns.
Another rises from the dead.

Lacking a dramatic guise
to test the wisdom of my love
(who's uncommitted can't deny),
I total up the virtues of

the gifted few who in the daze
of glory have risked nothing less
than everything that can be lost.
They take in payment all my praise.

The wind became a green idea.
The crows were out of place.
That color didn't suit their taste
or advance their bleak career.

The concept started to careen.
They pled a fervent case.
The wind became a green idea.
The crows were out of place.

It was wonderful to hear
them flaunt against their fate;
two shrill ascetics, born too late,
denounced the Technicolor leer.
The wind became a green idea.

From failing you can learn the grace
of falling well, from losing rise to be
the agile leaper of the tennis net,
an old king raging in the storm
or, anyhow, the smiler with a knife.

Not everyone can cut a dragon down to size,
live to be heir to tincan millions or
bed down with a favorite movie star,
slaphappy ever after. In the disaster
not everyone can save his skin.

Lucky in love and war are few
and far between. The scene must end
with the lesser corpses to be lugged before
lovers can dissolve in clinching bliss;
and many who bear witness wince

when, at last, a minor god appears,
a boy scout with a first-class noose,
to prove the miracle of matchless fire.
The rest will pass like ships at night—
cargo of unhatched chickens, pounds of flesh.

Still, to be beautiful among flashbulbs,
captured by tabloids, might be worse—
never to be able to deny three times
before the rooster crows, never to curse
perplexed successful Pilate face to face.

Fragment of a Tragedy

A messenger
        guiltless and eloquent arrives
        to speak in rhythm of catastrophe.
        The chorus, formal and self-conscious
        as a football team in a photograph,
        listens, translates in public language.

The Queen
        turns pale, mumbles the usual
        platitudes, and, with the lonely dignity
        of a dancer, disappears. She will die.
        The old king must also die. He enters,
        adjusting his fighting gear, awkward in armor

as a duck
        on dry land. His sons have all fallen
        and his daughters are resigned to fate.
        All generals have vanished. The Army
        is moving to the rear with the instinct
        of birds going South for the winter.

The King
        stops briefly, comments on the laws
        of man and nature and the vexing end
        things often come to. No god descends.
        He shrugs, and, as the curtain falls,
        salutes. At this point thundering applause.

The Angels

There are some things so beautiful
and strange the mind can't hold
them though it wrestles.

An angel sang in Caedmon's ears,
commanded his dumb thoughts to dance
and be articulate:

Sing me creation! And the kettle drums
the cymbals and the flaring horns
(though they were only words)

made wonders. The words arose
and, winged, ascended into light
where light is music.

The night is cold. The stars,
made brighter in the chill, still move
to tunes I listen for

where I walk thinking of Caedmon
and Jacob too, who choked
his answer from an angel.

The trees grasp for it and will be
filled in the morning with singing
birds. I go anxiously

remembering that truth is center
of all fables, and, fabulous,
the lightning of love

creates the angel and
the wrestler. Translate this parable.
It means to praise.

Dimensionless, they've left behind
buttons, daguerreotypes, a rusty sword
for a small boy to fondle, and the tales
he hears without believing a word

of the escapades of tall people.
The tight-lipped men with their beards
and their unsmiling women share the glint
of unreality. The facts he's heard

how this one, tamer of horses, fell
in a flourish of flags and roiling dust,
and one who met a dragon on the road,
and another, victim of strange lust,

changed into a pig with a ring tail,
fail to convince or bear the burden of
flesh and the wrestle for identity.
What he has never seen he cannot love,

though dutifully he listens.
Dismissed, he takes the sword and goes
campaigning in garden and arbor,
and in the henyard mighty blows

glisten in a tumult of feathers.
The hens cackle like grown-ups at tea
as he scatters them to the four winds.
The rooster, ruffled, settles in a tree

and crows his ancient reprimand.
"Let them stand up to me." The boy
thinks. "Let them be tall and terrible
and nothing less than kings." His joy

is all my sadness at the window
where I watch, wishing I could warn.
What can be said of the dead? They rise
to make you curse the day that you were born.

In the Hospital

Here everything is white and clean
as driftwood. Pain's localized
and suffering, strictly routine,
goes on behind a modest screen.

Softly the nurses glide on wheels,
crackle like windy sails, smelling of soap,
I'm needled and the whole room reels.
The Fury asks me how I feel

and, grinning turns to the brisk care
of an old man's need, he who awake
is silent, at the window stares,
sleeping, like drowning, cries for air.

And finally the fever like a spell
my years cast off. I notice now
nurse's firm buttocks, the ripe swell
of her breasts. It seems I will get well.

Next visitors with magazines;
they come whispering as in church.
The old man looks away and leans
toward light. Dying, too, is a routine.

I pack my bag and say goodbyes.
So long to nurse and this Sargasso Sea.
I nod to him and in his eyes
read, raging, the seabird's lonely cries.

I am five if I am one:
prophet walking on the sea,
hunter hiding in the tree,
serpent and the holy two.
I am five and I am none.
I am false and I am true.

I am tortured, torn apart.
Self-tormentor I know well
and for silver I would sell
one of me and seal by kiss
the sentence of a broken heart
and kill myself for less than this.

I am none and I am five.
I stalk the hunter hunting me.
I nail my body to a tree.
I swear and then deny. Although
flesh and bones will rise alive,
I will doubt myself, I know.

In North Carolina
the depth of promise is to learn
how, though the solid mountains lean
in every canting shower, disappear
in subtle fogs, they are still there
and will be for the eyes that keep
appointments with their architecture.

They are always moving, dazed and blue
above the landscape. The cold winds blow
adieus and fanfares through the mizzens
of the timberline, and only lessen
warmer, on the denser slopes,
the sense that everything is sailing.

Home is lower, looking up,
rapt and amazed to see them drop
dark shadows, which, like breaking waves
deluge the patterned valley, leave
rarely anything afloat, sweep
cornfields and cow pastures clean.

It takes faith to be fixed, to live
with so much happening and prove
nothing and simply be there always
moving and not moving. The truth allows
more changes than I might have hoped,
being perplexed by these perspectives.

Central Florida

Dark sang all the birds of Florida
in the hush which was like the hush
before sleep, the moment before music.

Everywhere the moon surged. The tide
gnawed at the edges of the fabulous peninsula
and the wind shuffled the palm fronds

like new money. But the real estate
was listening when all the birds sang,
in silence and contemplation and response,

in darkness to the darker song,
renewal (like the moon, the tide),
revival in a logic of echoes and equivalents.

Nothing is lost or won.
The sun shines as it has to
on the just and the unjust.
Rain falls on the false and true,
and what was beautiful is dust.

But wit, the amazing virtue,
"that sparkles while it wounds,"
endures now in the dance,
your parry and thrust of words
fenced in formal elegance.

We are accustomed to
barbwire, the searchlight glance,
explicitly indifferent,
and order's rare as innocence
viewed by victims of discontent.

This much has been proved:
the distance from here to truth
is light-years, reckoned by
wit or learned in wrath.
"'Tis better to laugh than to cry."

Milton's Adam

He first was all alone.
      Birds flashed in air
      and everywhere
bright creatures moved like smoke
in a light wind. Spoke
not to him nor tree nor stone.

He first knew loneliness
      who could not move
      toward any love
or by such learning be
hurt or whole. He
first of all touched emptiness.

He first was wholly lost
      dreaming her face,
      the form in space
her flesh would fill, her breath
of language and the death
that their duplicity would cost.

Outside the window dogwood snows
extravagantly pink and white. Inside
students are tracking Chaucer as he goes
a pilgrimage this season (as he must

yearly spring up and lead by hand
the wary and unwary toward
a Middle English promised land).
The students doze and nod in April daze.

Still, there's a robin on the path
to be transformed into
that heavy-breasted wench the Wife of Bath.
There's calm in brightness to recall

Griselda, perfect as a stone;
and there's the fever of the dogwood to
shiver you wholly skin and bone
which, in the same way, shivered Alysoun,

Fixed in this time of ice and fire,
instant for flowers and the chord
the wind makes of desire,
in quick profusion of the light,

you think: "Only the dead
are undistracted when the trees
burn brightly and each stone
is turned into a loaf of bread."

Orpheus

Spun out of thin air, these fictions
cry for the ears of a believer. Shards
of song fall in shining benediction
on the man who lives in a deck of cards.

I'd like to live always in a shower
of broken glass, in forests where flowers
thrive without expectation,
where each wish has a secret destination.

Hidden among angles of the hall
of mirrors, you'll find the answers to
perplexing questions. Words are scrawled
on the washroom wall. They are true.

Beauty, you see, is a stranger to
the beast; they will not meet
nor be defined until the true
from false is stripped, like bone from meat.

To be honest is to witness well.
To be faithful is to trust until
creation sings. While creatures riot,
wait for that chorus and be quiet.

And on the edge of April when the sun
almost, not quite, is ready to reach
over winter and to touch each
bud and seed, mind and buried god,
with intuitions and with ideas clad
in unexpected color, one hopes much.

Hoping is to teeter on an edge
of love, of promises and of decisions
made once and for all, of knowledge
viced in the mind. You vision
all doors opening at your touch,

and, thus corrupted, hoping dies
to be transformed. Now gods can rise
and flourish where there was not one.

From

The Sleeping Gypsy

(1958)

Buzzard

I've heard that holy madness is a state
not to be trifled with, not to be taken
lightly by jest or vow, by lover's token
or any green wreath for a public place. Flash
in the eyes of madmen precious fountains,
whose flesh is wholly thirst, insatiate.

I see this bird with grace begin to wheel,
glide in God's fingerprint, a whorl
of night, in light a thing burnt black,
unhurried. Somewhere something on its back
has caught his eye. Wide-winged he descends,
like angels, to the business of this world.

I've heard that saintly hermits, frail, obscene
in rags, slack-fleshed, with eyes like jewels, kneel
in dry sand, among the tortured mountains, feel
at last the torment of their prayers take shape,
take wings, assume the brutal rush of grace.
This bird comes then and picks those thin bones clean.

I've heard the case for clarity. I know
much can be said for fountains and for certain bells
that seem to wring the richness from the day
like juice of sweetest fruits, say, plums and tangerines,
grapes and pineapples and peaches. There are so many
ripe things, crushed, will sing on the thrilled tongue.

I know the architecture of the snow's composed
of multitudes of mirrors whose strict forms
prove nothing if they do not teach that God loves all
things classic, balanced and austere in grace
as, say, Tallchief in *Swan Lake,* a white thing floating
like the feather of a careless angel, dropped.

But there are certain of God's homely creatures that
I can love no less—the shiny toad, a fine hog fat in mud,
sporting like Romans at the baths, a mockingbird
whose true song is like oboes out of tune, a crow
who, cawing above a frozen winter field,
has just the note of satire and contempt.

I will agree that purity's a vital matter,
fit for philosophers and poets to doze upon, agree
the blade is nobler than a rock. But then I think
of David with Goliath, how he knelt
and in a cloudy brook he felt for stones.
I like that disproportion. They were well thrown.

A rolling stone gathers no moss.

This is the simple truth: e.g. the rock
of Sisyphus (so lichenless it gleams
like a bald man in the sun) it seems
will never have a moment on its back

to sigh and stretch and feel a fine
green growing like a handstitched lace
among the honored piles in public place.
Few of us can mellow like good wine,

age into some gracious Judgment Day
in caves as nice as any Plato thought;
but, daily sold and daily bought,
are judged and juggled, rolled away

as smooth and nude as grapes on vine.
Still, there's pleasure in the constant dance
of things. Many will sparkle and by chance
a lone stone like a diamond shine.

You can't make a silk purse out of a sow's ear.

On the contrary, it appears
that truth is always in disguise.
Take, for example, the careers
of gods in flesh, so camouflaged,

they blend into the texture of
our sweaty dreams of sweatless enterprise;
or those tall heroes who for love
fall on all fours and howl like cats

in heat. This proves the silk
can be converted, you surmise,
but not the negative. We milk
this world (says Wilbur) but we don't believe.

I say that, blest, all water turns to wine.
I say there's more than meets the eye
when Salome, veil by veil, her fine
clothes peels to the essential skin

and bones. There are two thieves.
One of them spits and shuts his eyes.
The other, seeing truth so naked, grieves
and finds himself in paradise.

You can't plant peach pits and grow pear trees.

A man is more than sum of all his deeds.

Say that the finest actions could be kept
like flowers pressed in pages, say that doom
is totalled from a column of calm figures,
the dark and light, the services and sins,

until there comes in fire a single answer,
ineffaceable and indisputable, what then?
There are heroes for whom horses wept
and stones, and how shall frail perfume

from antique flowers guard a noble gesture,
though multitude of ghosts may haunt the tomb?
Grass grows rich where white Adonis stepped,
and from the bones of Orpheus, bright as pins,

poems sprout still like grain from quickened seeds.

Some Notes on Aesop

The donkey in the lion's skin
    I take this tale to prove
    much that we love and fear
    is false when tried by speech;

    for only the lion should roar,
    as cooing becomes the dove
    and a peach is a peach is a peach.

    But those whom hungers move
    to sail for unknown shores
    or taste of fruit beyond their reach,

    must take the donkey for
    a wise beast and approve
    what he was trying to teach.

The raven and the fox
    As usual, the fox is right.
    And flattery's a terrible swift sword
    and vanity a wound that doesn't heal.

    But what was (in truth) the case?
    Wasn't the chance that once,
    just once, the raven's voice

    would be seized by a marvelous tune
    worth any morsel of food
    and the sight of the satisfied fox?

The tortoise and the hare
    If standing at the finish line
    wreathed in flowers and/or smiles
    for newspapers is what
    counts, the moral's fine.

If such persistence is correct
praise the spider and the ant.
Fiddling grasshoppers can't
please Aesop's Architect.

But God knows there's a place
for those who for pure joy
run and fall asleep
while solemn others win a race.

Be uncorrupted all, uprooted quite
from gnarling, grasp and grope.
Be straightened like uncoiling rope
spun whistling over water clean as sight.

Move urgently to mooring. Small
is a shadow, neither monster nor
exactly twin, tugging your toes, sprawled
like a drowned man on the ocean floor

whom tempest and tirade can never reach
to stir to action, torment into song.
In darkness lean towards light. Beseech
new blossomings to happen and the strong

ship, wave-whipped, safely to arrive
in harbor where loves like green leaves thrive.

1.

She was a dazzle.
How her words flew!
Like strange birds.

Who could capture
the fury of their wings
or their fierce songs?

Where I've planted
nothing will grow.
Nothing prospers.

Let dark birds come
now and find me.
Pluck out my eyes.

2.

My joy was joyless.
Her bright smile was
a pair of shears.

So rare her flesh!
But at my touch
she turned to stone.

All I can harvest
is crop of bruises.
Mouthful of chaff.

Pity the hunter
whose bowstring is slack.
Limp arrows in quiver.

3.
My love was rich.
Golden her body.
Coins for her eyes.

My love was treasure.
I was a pirate.
Faulty the map.

For crown I wear
thorns. For bread
I taste fists.

Find me a willow.
I'll show that tree
how to bear fruit.

4.
My love lay fallow.
Dust on her lips.
Green in my eyes.

My love was sleeping.
I stormed her dream
in the tall tower.

My love's a garden.
Wild children grow
calm in her hands.

My love is holy.
It would be prayer
to praise her in words.

I've heard some jealous women say
that if your skin were cut away
and tacked upon a public wall
it would not please the eyes at all.

They say your bones are no great prize,
that, hanging in the neutral breeze,
your rig of ribs, your trim of thighs
would catch no fetching harmonies

but tinkle like a running mouse
over piano keys. They hold
that, stripped, your shabby soul
will whimper like a vacant house

you are so haunted. "Ask
her," they say, "if she'll unmask.
Let her shed beauty like the winter trees.
Time will bring her to her knees."

Still, I must have you as you are,
all of a piece, beautiful and vain,
burning and freezing, near and far,
and all my joy and all my pain.

And if you live to scrub a floor
with prayer, to weep like a small ghost,
which of us will suffer more,
who will be wounded most?

PROFESSOR OF BELLES LETTRES

His book-lined study ought to be a TV set.
Some very nice first editions in alphabetical order
    and himself fully armed by J. Press,
chainsmoking while he conducts a class—
"The Growth of National Consciousness in American Lit."

There's a picture window with a view
of barbered green lawn and a man with a lawn mower.
"Italians love to cut grass," his wife said.

Afterwards there is tea
during which he collects
the latest undergraduate slang
in an indexed notebook.

I do not know if he believes in anything
or has any love by which he lives,
but, over the shine of the teacups
and the glint of the silver service,

I have seen tears in his eyes
when he talked about Sacco and Vanzetti
    or the peace of Walden Pond.

GADFLY

At the Faculty Meeting I saw him bleed
for Nonconformity and, good classicist, bare
all his wounds, calling on us to rise, rebel,
to shrug the yoke, come down from bitter cross.

    The President, I noticed, was impassive,
    attentive and indifferent as a *croupier*.
    Not the least fault or fissure of emotion
    troubled the contours of his familiar smile.

Now this is Ancient History.
We live and learn.

The Gadfly was promoted while
Rebels were scattered like a covey of quail
in everywhich direction.
Folding their caps and gowns like Arab tents,
they muttered "tar and feathers," fled.

Now over coffee, steaming rich
subsistence of the academic nerve,
I hear him say: "What we need
is less of milk and honey and more sting.
Things hereabouts are whitewashed. Let us
act. A little water clears us of the deed.
  And what do *you* think?"

I smile and shrug.
I pay the check and plead a class
and leave him talking still,
safe in the shadow of his Great Man,
a trim Diogenes in tub of honest tweed.

PEDANT

Privately, your pencil makes
wry marginalia, doodles at the edge
of noted pages, underlines examples of
what you call the worst excesses.

"Puddles of sentiment!" You scrawl
an epitaph for Shelley and his critics,
being uneasy among the vague Romantics.

"Pope & Swift would have admired
  Bentley & Dennis
if *only* they had understood."
Thus gladly reconcile and make a peace
among the factions of your favorite century.

If I hide my mouth to laugh,
if I yawn, doze while you drone,
if, choking on my imprecision,
I curse you in the language of those years
for "a Blockhead and a Fine Dull Ass,"
I must (in truth) confess

your strictness is like a conscience,
your rigor's like the pattern which
the feet must follow in numbered silence
before they waltz free to real music.

One learns to count before one learns the dance.
One learns to speak grammatically before
one takes the stance of satire and/or praise.

And I have seen the virtue of
your passion for precision.
You teach, by vehement revision,
that labor is a way to love.

All uncompelled, weightless as the notes
wrung out of bells at kindling dawn,
more light-thrilled than a shallow stream
over brute rock dashed, these thoughts
flash to song like figures from a dream.

Creation roars. Happens in fire and flood
the riot which is God. A flock of hurts
(the sad crowd, grazing of bitter hearts,
the blank gaze, fright in the rotten wood)
released, reprieved, departs

as, naked, empty as a broken bowl
of everything save light and air, I learn
to praise the water, praise the fire. Burns
then, eternal phoenix, all the soul
I was, and I rejoice to be reborn.

Swift has been misunderstood, his rage
called everything but simple honesty,
the buzzing in his brain identified
as everything but the lightning of God.

Now scholars nod over the burning page,
with pencils poised, fidget and warble
their footnotes wild, and Stella is
and she isn't, and God knows

Swift had marbles in his head—
tall sculptured figures posing there,
naked and shining, the image of
the rare and endless possibility of man.

Follow him, if you can, with eyes
wide open. Sketch for a skeptic age
the contours of his anger and his love.
Be humble if he, furious, replies.

Speak to us who
are also split.
Speak to the two
we love and hate.

You have been both
and you have known
the double truth
as, chaste, obscene,

you were the lover
and the loved.
You were the giver
who received.

Now tell us how
we can be one
another too.
Speak to us who

in single wrath
cannot be true
to life or death.
Blinder than you.

Martha Graham: Appalachian Spring

Our blue mountains are vague as smoke. In April we dream we are awake. Our dreams are pink and white like dogwood and as sweet as rock candy.

Then the Devil comes walking like a bear on his hind legs, and his fiddler sets everything to dancing. O Martin Luther, O Jack Calvin, can't you keep those tunes out of my ears? In April, in May, the Devil makes his music like a fat bumblebee in the flowers.

Thank the Lord, the long dry summer days come along after.

The Magi

First they were stiff and gaudy,
three painted wooden figures on the table,
bowing in a manger without any walls
among bland clay beasts and shepherds
who huddled where my mother always put them
in a perfect ring around the Hold Child.
At that season and by candlelight
it was easy for a child to believe in them.

Later on I *was* one. I brought gold,
ascended the platform of the Parish House
and muffed my lines, but left my gift
beside the cheap doll in its cradle,
knelt in my fancy costume trying to look wise
while the other two (my friends and rivals
for the girl who was chosen to be Mary)
never faltered with frankincense and myrrh.

Now that was a long time ago.
And now I know them for what they were,
moving across vague spaces on their camels,
visionaries, madmen, poor creatures possessed
by some slight deviation of the stars.
I know their gifts were shabby, if symbolic.
Their wisdom was a thing of waking dreams.
Their robes were dirty and their breath was bad.

Still, I would dream them back.
Let them be wooden and absurd again
in all the painted glory that a child
loved. Let me be one of them.
Let me step forward once more awkwardly
and stammer and choke on my prepared speech.
I will bring gold again and kneel
foolish and adoring in the dungy straw.

Grapes

In Tuscany
where I was a soldier for a while
the grapes were wonderful on hillsides.
They grew and glistened in the light.
They dreamed all season long
the tuneful dreams of Tuscany.

And they clotted & clustered & swelled
and they spilled over like fountains
green & shining everywhere you looked

until in tidal waves they broke
over the stranded barbwire
flooding pillboxes foxholes & minefields

stalling tanks & trucks
disrupting wire communications
and even carried away the CP tent.

By Christ we got drunk!
We drank and drank
and drank the blood
        of Tuscany.

And reeling in that holy light
        of Tuscany
we dreamed that all the towers leaned
        in Tuscany.

I like the version of Aristophanes,
the story he tells in the *Symposium,*
how we were altogether once and how,
ripped apart, uncoupled, sundered,
we are the lost and naked halves,
and how we dream of that wholeness
as, say, a man who's lost a leg
sometimes feels the joy of his missing limb
springing, dancing, running . . .
and other times he feels it longing
to belong to him again. I don't know
which of these is the greater torment.

The other story, how in dreamy Eden
Adam lost a rib without a wound
and woke to find a stranger he could love,
is too stern for the banquet scene.
I was there. Stood in that garden.
I named the birds, the beasts, the trees.
I tasted the joys of that forbidden apple.
I remember the core was bitter in my mouth
and when I spat the seeds they grew into barbwire.
I heard the thunder of God's kettle drums.
Wounded then, at last, I took your hand.
And we are still together.

Bathing Beauty

The sun, this morning
scored for trumpets, blares
over the sculptured gestures of
bathers in scanty costumes.

They are untouched.
Only the gulls and children fly
for pure joy to the holy noise.
Older we warm by the tune

like the blind by a dying
fire. Cat-sleek, curled
in knowledge of herself,
dozing in the dazzle,

she has caught my eye.
I see her on a scallop shell
or lounging in the perfect lines
of a Matisse.

O Suzanna, I'll
stand on tiptoes, breathless
among the frozen elders. O
Judith, here's my head,

my heart, my four limbs,
and my balls and all
(O Ruth) my alien corn.
She stretches, sighs, and seems

to be asleep. I shut my eyes
to hear the gulls and children
sing. I hear my voice
wailing by an ancient wall.

The sun, all trumpets, blares
and the tide is falling, falling
like the walls of Jericho
whose waves are tongues of dust.

From

Abraham's Knife

(1961)

Rape of the Sabines

(a frieze in the Roman Forum)

It seems to be a kind of dance,
graceful, almost stylish in the way
some of the victims are carried high,
slight ballerinas swooning in the arms
of men whose grip is less than gruff.

One is running, sure enough.
She's half-naked already, and real harm
is a step and the length of a hand away.
Though he will have her by and by,
there's a hint of pleasure in her wince

as if she acted in the trance-
like state of dreams where dire alarms
are set to music. My grownup's eye
is a ghostly witness. Play
of children is composed of just such stuff

and nonsense, threat and bluff.
We may have been a race of dancers once,
I think, before we tried to come to terms
with what is truth and what is clearly lie.
We went stark naked night and day.

Now it's pure folly to obey
an impulse just to stand and sigh
(at whose doors the real wolves huff and puff)
for that lost childhood and its charms,
its equal parts of rape and sheer romance.

The crows, a hoarse cone in the wind,
a swarm of flies, so small and busy
they seem, so tossed by breeze
from mountains where the snow
glitters like a brooding skullcap,
the crows, I say, swirl and cry out
and rise to be torn apart in tatters,
a shower of burnt cinders, fall
in one swoop to a perch in the sun
on the lee side of a Grecian temple.

Sheep too. Soft music of light
bells. I've seen them grazing
in other ruins, cropping shadowed grass
among the broken emblems of empire,
and once with the dome of St. Peter's
for background, behind and above them
like a gas balloon on a string.
There behind me posed Garibaldi,
bronze above a squalling traffic circle.
Now crows and sheep and a yawning guard

share the ruins of Paestum with me.
The wind off the mountains chills
and westward the sea is white-capped too,
is all of sparkling like new coins.
"And they came nigh unto the place
and there builded a great city."
To what end? That a Greek relic
should tug the husband and wife
from snug *pensione* with camera and guidebook?
For a few tinkling sheep and the exploding crows?

I am uneasy among ruins, lacking
the laurel of nostalgia, romantic wand,
and cannot for a purpose people empty places
with moral phantoms, ghostly celebrations.
I listen to the soft bells, watch

the crows come to life again, sheer
off and fall to wrestling the wind,
thinking: "If sheep may safely stand
for that which, shorn and dipped,
is naked bleating soul, why then

I take these crows (whose name
is legion) for another of the same:
the dark, the violent, the harsh,
lewd singers of the dream, scraps
of a shattered early urn, cries
cast out, lost and recovered, all
the shards of night. Cold air
strums the fretted columns and
these are the anguished notes
whose dissonance is half my harmony."

When the great gray European dark
settles on the city like a spell,
the streetlights haloed, the old people
huddled in doorways, eyes alert,
and my heart sags in a net of veins
like a rock in a sling (for History
is the giant here, stretches and straddles
the dark continent), and I walk home
and would go on tiptoe if I could
so as not to break anything,
not to kiss dust from anybody's lips
or change anything from stone to flesh,

then, by God, I see the lovers,
the Roman lovers on the walk,
leaning together, he whispering,
she listening, laughing, so close
you can't separate their shadows.
O Noah's pairs of all creation
couldn't please me more! I hurl
my heart against the night
and hear the astounded giant fall.
And I rejoice. I fumble with a key
and open doors. I kiss my wife
and hold my children hostage in my arms.

Egyptian Gold

> Just as the Egyptians had not only idols and grave
> burdens which the people of Israel detested and
> avoided, so also they had vases and ornaments of
> gold and silver and clothing which the Israelites
> took with them secretly as they fled, as if to put
> them to a better use.
>
> —St. Augustine, *On Christian Doctrine*

The pickpockets of Rome
are clever as any of their kind
I've ever known. They can
lift the wallet from your pocket
with less touch than a breeze.
They can disembowel a pocketbook
while it hangs, idle, on a lady's arm,
and she'll never know it until,
home with a sigh, she flings
it on a table where it lies
like a cleaned fish. And when
they work in pairs and trios,
as, for example, in the Stazione Termini,
it's with the precision of the ballet.
They thrive on difficulty.
Button your coat, hold your pocketbook
like a new baby, and nevertheless
your property is theirs if they
have a mind to have it.

But private property isn't
our only topic just now.
I don't own much, it's true,
and it isn't likely that either
pickpockets or poets
will ever be rich enough to care.

The point is:
What happens when you fall among thieves?
And who, Lord, is my neighbor?

(Jesus Christ, who knew one thief
from another, had the answer
for a lawyer to ponder on.
A hard saying. There's only one
Samaritan. The rest of us
lie naked and beaten in the ditch.)
Now in an age when thievery
is so refined it calls itself
success, and to be stripped and beaten
is to be foxed, and all grapes
go to the vineyard keeper,
and nobody, early or late,
draws any wages, and we applaud
the blind man leading the blind,
I feel like saying with P. T. Barnum—
"This Way To The Egress!"

But then I call to mind
St. Augustine glossing Exodus,
explaining why God gave permission
for Moses to take along Egyptian gold
and showing how this means
that all things are to God.
And if we're going to build
new temples we might as well
use the marble of the pagans.
And if we're going to tell the truth
we'd better gut the pocketbooks
of all the poets who've tried and failed.
As we pass their honored biers
we'll pick the pennies from their eyes.

I'm pleased by these Roman pickpockets.
As I said, they never get rich,
and finally their fingers lose the art
and stiffen out of subtlety
just as sweet singers grow hoarse.
And they end up wistful on corners

watching the new generation strut
sassy and unplucked past them.
As long as they don't take my passport,
I'll praise them and their skill.

But I don't want to leave the impression
of a typical American overseas
and overawed by all that's foreign.
My grandfather lost his good gold watch
in an elevator at the Waldorf.

I think Caravaggio has seen it right,
shown it anyway with the boy and the head
(Is it really his *own* face, the giant's,
slack-jawed, tormented? Another story.)
the look of the lean boy, the lips
pursed to spit or kiss, the head held
at arm's length from him by the hair,
the eyes, if they read anything, showing
pity and contempt, hatred and love,
the look we keep for those we kill.
He will be king. Those fingers twined
in dark will pluck the hair of harps,
golden, to sing the measure of our joy
and anguish. By the hair will Absalom
dangle from a limb, his tongue a thoroughfare
for flies, and a man grown old and soft
will tear *his* from the roots to make lament.
The look you give Goliath on that day
will flicker on your weathered face
when you spy bare Bathsheba on the roof
(O the dark honey, liquor of strange flesh,
to turn a head to birds, a heart to stone!)
And you will live to learn by heart
the lines upon this alien face.
So I think that Caravaggio
saw it right, that at the moment when
the boy has killed the man and lifts the head
to look at it is the beginning and the end.
I, who have pictured this often and always
stopped short of the miracle, seen David stoop
and feel for smooth stones in the filmy brook,
the instant when palm and fist
close like a beggar's on a cold coin,
know now that I stopped too soon.
Bathed in light, this boy is bound

to be a king. But the sword . . .
I had forgotten that. A slant
of light, its fine edge rests across
his thigh. Never again a rock will do.
It fits his hand like a glove.

Bubbles

Not like we used to with pipes,
which combined the pleasures of
pretending we were smoking with
the chance of a mouthful of soap,

but nowadays with a seagreen liquid,
bottled, and a spoon-shaped eyelet
with a handle. You dip it
and in a wave you have

a room that's full of bubbles.
Round and rich they catch the light
in square small patches of color,
and they hover, float and fall

and pop. My children are
pleased and puzzled. It's new
to them. They snatch at globes
to find their hands are empty

and the bubble's gone.
Let some stern moralist take on
the task of making sense of this.
I never could explain why balloons

burst and playing-card towers fall.
I say they're beautiful to see,
however made, by pipe or wand,
and not to have.

Kings might have given ransom
to own an air so jeweled and clear,
so nothing-filled and handsome.
Children, there are no kings here.

A Toast for the Bride and Groom

I raise my glass of wine,
but how shall I confine
in words the music of
this captured light? Love
dances free, will not keep still.
Can grapes, so crushed and chill,
contain a calendar of sunny days?
Can empty cups be filled with praise?

I know a list of famous cups
once tasted, once turned up
and drained to the last dregs,
could make you shiver like the legs
of a new colt. Down on their knees
dropped Circe's drinkers. Socrates
proved bitter can be sweetest good.
There's one that turns the wine to blood.

There's another of that kind
that once made water into wine,
and that's the one I wish for
now. Glass, be a metaphor.
Wine, be symbolic, and my toast
be shy and sudden as a ghost.
What's unsaid is all history.
"Our glasses brim with mystery."

Who won't be passionate and brave
dressed as a musketeer, a sly
rapier taut along his thigh?

Who's as exotic as the slave,
the white one, she whom the sheik's
least oriental gesture turns as weak-

kneed as a new calf? Here's
Antoinette, the sport-
ing queen and, there, the short

man's idol, the Napoleon
of bangs, and a hidden hand.
All in this company may comprehend

the joys of Proteus, the complex
pieties of masks, a face
that's not for long. Without a trace

survivors of the shipwreck disappear,
replaced by grinning cannibals. Forget
not yet the Space Cadet,

he to whom moon and stars
are near and known. Nor
ignore Eve whose leaves implore

an Adam to be tempted one more time.
(The hopeful pathos of her eyes
is not concealed by the disguise.)

But pity's in the aftermath:
costume for mothballs, gilt
by water gone, the sword at hilt

clean broken. Who believes
that gods in flesh have changed
the dead to quick, familiar to the strange?

Goodbye, Old Paint, I'm Leaving Cheyenne

for Roy Waldau

From my television set come shots and cries,
the hollow drum of hooves and then,
emerging from the snow of chaos, the tall riders
plunging in a tumultuous surf of dust.
The Stage, it seems, is overdue.
My children, armed to the teeth, enchanted,
are, for the moment at least, quiet.
I see the Badmen riding for the Gulch,
all grins, not knowing as we do
("The rest of you guys follow me.")
the Hero's going to get there first.
And as the plot, like a lariat, spins out
its tricky noose, I shrink to become
a boy with a sweaty nickel in his palm
waiting to see two features and a serial
at the Rialto on Saturday morning:
Buck Jones, the taciturn, Tom Mix
of spinning silver guns and a splendid horse,
and somebody left face to face with a buzz saw,
to writhe until next Saturday morning.

But how you have changed, my *chevaliers,*
how much we have all grown up!
No Hero now is anything but cautious.
(We know the hole a .45 can make.)
No Badman's *born* that way.
("My mother loved me but she died.")
No buzz saw frightens like the whine
of a mind awry. No writhing's like
the spirit's on its bed of nails.
I clench my nickel tighter in my fist.
Children, this plot is new to me.
I watch the Hero take the wrong road
at the Fork and gallop away, grim-faced,
weary from the exercise of choice.
I see the Badmen safely reach the Gulch,
then fight among themselves and die
to prove good luck is worse than any wound.

My spellbound children smile and couldn't care
less about my fit of pure nostalgia
or all the shabby ghosts I loved and lost.

Fat Man

O flesh, my tyrant wife, my shrew,
old slattern, what's to become of you?
Of *us?* It's true I've come to hate
the way you smirk from mirrors, float
in steaming tubs, sweat on summer days,
or, shameless, writhe in nets of eyes
that measure all your bulk and girth.

What is to love? To love's to dance.
The spirit leads the flesh. Without a wince
the flesh should follow and should smile.
A map of all of you shows miles
of frowns. I study you and weep
for pity's sake—the only crop I reap.
I'll never leave you, cruel and fair,
who leave me panting halfway up the stair.

Once hand and wrist and eye
were silent partners
quick as gulls.
Never a thought,
no bar between.

Cast lines where I pleased.
And I hauled in
sag and squirm,
the groan of plenty
bending my tackle.

Now luck's a total stranger.
My eye is tricked
by false horizons.
Hand and wrist
won't dance together.

Dark birds cry the names
of drowned men,
pick to bones
my meager catch.
Only thought groans.

But that's one kind of music.
Let flesh wither
in this total war.
Can still spit and cast off
in any weather.

Face like an old fighter's
    (that is, hurt)
a bad cough and the color
    of jailhouses
nothing to do with himself
    but hang around
gas stations post office and
    the railroad depot
watching arrivals & departures
    yawn like a cat.

Face like Roman stone
    (that is brute)
chipped and broken nose
    eyes vague
crude hands quick to take
    a cigarette
but too slack to make
    a fist nowadays
Jesus loves him this I know
    who else can?

Snapshot: Ambassadress

We had a parade for the lady near Livorno.
I spent a solid hour shining on my boots.

We got there and lined up,
      eight thousand men,
and waited quite a while because she was late.
Finally she showed up and rode up and down
trooping the line in a white jeep.
She said America would be proud of us
and what an important job we'd done in Trieste.

After it was all over and we were back in the tents,
a man in my squad (he was from Alabama) asked me:
"Say, Sarge, who in the hell *was* that Clara Bell Lou
      we fell out for?"

Snapshot: Politician

When I attended the funeral
he was more solemn and tiptoeing
than even the undertaker.
        For Christ's sake!

He had a great big hand and a good word
for everybody. He was driven in
an air-conditioned Cadillac.

His hair was black, luxuriant and curly
        as the wool on a ram.
And when he *did* smile it was like all the lights
        of a Christmas tree going on at once.

At the grave, just after the coffin was lowered
(it went down so quickly, quietly, it was astonishing),
somebody asked him about a speeding ticket.

"My word's good as far as the Savannah River,"
he said. "After that you're in the hands
        of Herman Talmadge."

When the elders found me I was not Susanna. I turned to stone.

I was transfigured, gored and tossed in their eyes. When I felt
what they were thinking my body turned to stone.
  O Susanna, don't you cry for me
  In New Orleans, land of dreams

Take me in your hands. I swear I'll come to life again. I'm
just like a fish out of water, a birdie in a cage. Take me in your
hands and all of me will smile and dance for you.
  Pretty birdie, sing me a tune
  In New Orleans, land of dreams

My lips taste dust. But, ah, my flesh is cool and fragile as the rain.
I am the Sleeping Beauty. No one can ever wake me. Be kind . . .
  O Susanna, don't you cry for me

Now chaos has pitched a tent
in my pasture, a circus tent
like a huge toadstool
in the land of Giants. Oh,
all night long the voices of
the damned and saved keep me
awake and, *basso,* the evangelist.
Fire & brimstone, thunder & lightning,
telegrams in the unknown tongue.
The bushes are crawling with couples.
I see one girl so leafy that
she might be Daphne herself.

I know there were Giants once,
one-eyed wonders of the morning
world. Ponderous, they rode
dinosaurs like shetland ponies,
timber for toothpicks, boulders for
baseballs, oceans for bathtubs,
whales for goldfish. Great God,
when they shook fists and roared,
stars fell down like snowflakes
under glass! Came then Christ
to climb the thorny beanstalk,
and save us one and all.

ARE YOU SAVED????
Rocks are painted, trees nailed
with signs, fences trampled.
Under the dome of the tent
falls salt of sweat and tears
enough to kill my grass at the roots.
Morning and I'll wake to find
the whole thing's gone. Bright dew
and blessed silence. Nothing

to prove they camped here and tried
to raise a crop of hell except
that scar of dead space (where the tent was)
like a huge footprint.

Night Poem: U.S.A.

They roll up the sidewalks all over town
by 11:30 p.m. Lord, by midnight there's nothing
doing, moving. Lone streetlights glare
like one-eyed giants, do not dare to dance.
Here and there a late place burns pale
fire to keep back the beasts of the night.
Somebody's sick, you think (like Huck),
or, less innocent, project the lewd
fantastic, the cheap frail beams
of poor Imagination gone awry
into those naked rooms. Alas
for the cop on the corner who gives you
a glass-eyed stare, and for the last car
weaving the pavement like a lonesome drunk.
Dancers, giants, heroes and dreamers,
where are you now? It's a fact—
when the heart breaks it doesn't make a sound.

Where hills are hard and bare,
rocks like thrown dice, heat
and glare that's clean and pitiless,
a shadow dogs my heels, limp
as a drowned man washed ashore.
True sacrifice is secret, none
to applaud the ceremony, nor
witness to be moved to tears.
No one to see. God alone
knows, Whose great eye winks not,
from Whom no secrets are hid.

My father, I have loved you,
love you now, dead all these years.
Your ghost shadows me home.
Your laughter and your anger still
trouble my scarecrow head like wings.
My own children, sons and daughter, study
my stranger's face. Their flesh,
bones frail as a small bird's,
is strange, too, in my hands.
What will become of us?
I read my murder in their eyes.

And you, old father Abraham,
my judge and executioner, I pray
be witness to me now. I ask
some measure of your faith. Forgive
us, Jew and Gentile, all
your children, all your victims.
In naked country of no shadow
your hand is raised in shining arc.
And we are fountains of foolish tears
enough to flood and green a world again.
Strike for my heart. Your blade is light.

For My Sons

This world that you're just beginning
now to touch, taste, feel, smell, hear and see,
castled in enigma, and daily more and more
finding sounds in your throats, tremors on tongue
to play with, words (some like a ripe plum
or an orange to daze the whole mouth
with sweetness, so that in speaking
you seem to kiss, some like a bitter phlegm
to be hawked up and spit out clean), the world
is all I would claim for you, save you from.

I am a foolish father like all the rest,
would put my flesh, my shadow in between
you and the light that wounds and blesses.
I'd throw a cloak over your heads
and carry you home, warm and close, to keep
you from the dark that chills to the bone.
Foolish (I said), I'd teach you only words
that sing on the lips. Still, you have to learn
to spit in my face and save your souls.
Still you must curse with fever and desire.

Nothing of earned wisdom I can give you,
nothing save the old words like rock candy
to kill the taste of dust on the tongue.
Nothing stings like the serpent, no pain greater.
Bear it. If a bush should burn and cry out,
bow down. If a stranger wrestles, learn his name.
And if after long tossing and sickness you find
a continent, plant your flags, send forth a dove.
Rarely the fruit you reach for returns your love.

Fig Leaves

At times sick of the dishonesty of men
to men, the lies that lie in the mouth
like tongues (O fluttering of tongues
like the snapping of flags in the wind!) . . .
At times sick unto death of myself
and the lies I tell myself, waking, walking,
sleeping, dreaming, lies that must choke,
gag me like a drunk man's vomit
until I lie (indeed) on the ground,
face the color of a bruise, arms and legs
kicking vain signals like a roach on its back . . .
I could crack my pen in two like a bone,
a thin bone, wishbone, meatless, chewed
down to the slick and bitter surface.
Better my tongue were a dead leaf
(just so dry, to be bitten to powder).
Better my ears were stone, my pen
at least a hoe, a shovel, a plough,
any good servant of growing things.
Better our sole flag were fig leaves
at least to salute the mercy of God
when in the cool of the evening He came
(Adam and Eve on trembling shanks
squatted and hoped to be hidden)
and cursed us out of the garden.
But not before we learned
to wear our first costume
(seeing the truth was a naked shame),
to lie a little and live together.

Solitaire

The days shuffle together.
Cards again? No, no, I mean
like convicts in lockstep, like
the patients on the Senile Ward
I saw once, gray and feeble,
blank-eyed creatures in cheap cotton,
pumped full of tranquilizers—
"It's really the efficient way to handle
the situation," an attendant told me—
so lethargic they could hardly pick up their feet.

The gray days shuffle together.
The trees are picked and plucked,
sad tough fowl not fit for stewing.
The round world's shaved and hairless
like the man in the moon. Screams,
but you can't hear it. Next door
the dog howls and I can.
Break out a fresh deck for God's sake!
Bright kings and queen and one-eyed jacks.
Free prisoners. Let the old men go home.

From

For a Bitter Season

(1967)

Old Man Waking

Something hoots.
An owl, a freight train or
a rusty tramp, hull down in harbor.

I wake up in a strange land.

Last night I dreamed it all again.
The trees were green as paper money.
The fruit in the leaves was candy
and the grapes had grown so fat and rich
to look at them was to be dizzy drunk.
Birds sang in the leaves and the leaves
leaned together to gossip in whispers.

And you were there
so young and fair
and shining that my heart
like a raw recruit
stumbled to salute.

Then you walked toward me.
The dew on the grass glittered
and the blades of grass parted
before your bare feet like
an armed mob struck dumb
by a pair of fine ladies
naked, soft, and beautiful.

You smiled as you offered me a peach.
I ate it all and threw the pit away.
When I looked again
the teeth of your smile were gone
and you were as old as sin.
Flesh of dried figs,
eyes of phlegm,
feet shod in callouses.
Your face went away too,
a smear of candlewax.

I have forgotten your right name.

Something hoots
insistent and derisive
and I wake in a strange land.

I curse the mirror on the wall.
I have lost every key I ever owned.
Now I will dress myself and go forth,
armed with a terrible temper and a walking cane.

Children,
bright children quicker than birds,
whose eyes are coins of light,
whose laughter is the source of music,
children, come taste my knuckles
and the hard shiny tips of my boots.

Rainy Day

It is raining hard today and the girls that I teach
come to class, lightly over the wet lawn, barefoot.
A corner of the room sprouts a garden of umbrellas.

One stops by the door to dry her feet,
hand propped on the frame to keep her balance.
Her foot is small and soft, delicate yet sturdy.

One small sturdy hand pressed against the door frame.
Small sturdy suntanned legs. She stands on one leg
and crosses the other as simply as a bird.

I am pleased. All this time and I didn't even know
you had a foot, young lady, flat sole and little toes
to go to market with or run squealing all the way home.

I am troubled, too. Off balance, I feel
the intimate shiver of the elders in the garden
when young Susanna gently let her garments fall.

God knows I am too old for it, knows
I have a job to do and children of my own to feed.
Let me disappear. I shrink and vanish

into a camouflage of colorful umbrellas.
Now they have turned into mushrooms,
magic toadstools glistening with rain.

And in just a minute my students will run past me,
skimming the wet grass on swift naked feet.
Won't one of you stop and pick a toadstool?

And sleep forever in a shining spell?
Though the world goes gray, be always pink?
Though old men lust, smile in your sweet dream?

A bell is ringing. I find my hands are opening
a book. Rain falls outside and I look
into a flowering of blank pretty faces.

I have seen one face, so beautiful it made me sing,
fall to ruin in a cracked looking glass. And I have felt
time print crow's feet at the edges of my own eyes.

So much, then, for the glitter of rain, the shining lawn,
a garden of toadstools, faces like flowers and one bare foot
I should have kissed for joy. "Let us take up where

we left off yesterday. . . ."

Virtuosity

(Bernini's Apollo & Daphne)

I see the girl become a tree,
fear printed cleanly on her face,
lips tense with a frozen scream.

From her toes roots reach for earth.
Leaves from her fingers flutter free
to test a breeze which is her clothing.

She is made of marble much like flesh,
veined in blue and polished to a point
where mortal hands are sorely tempted.

Bernini, virtuoso, tortured her
into this being and, as well,
the slim, lightfooted god a step behind.

I think: What virtue is in this?
Marble is not flesh and blood.
I love the grain of naked lumber.

But here she is, in fact, who first
was wholly stone and now seems flesh
and in one shudder will be wood.

Even the god must be baffled
by richness of change and becoming,
by the anguish of answered prayer.

My prayers stop in my throat.
I dream of our lost beginnings.
I huddle in poor skin and bones.

Think of Bernini, then. Praise him.
His joyous hands were simply free.
Here prayers are songs from Eden.

I had a dream of purity.

From weight of flesh and cage of bone,
it was I who was set free
and that other me like a blown weed
was scattered by the wind. Frail bones
(They were so small and light to carry
so much hunger and fury.)
crumbled into finest dust
and the wind took that away too.
And last of all my mouth, my lips,
a red yawn, a taut shriek, my tongue
fluttered like a dead leaf and vanished.
And then it was I who was free,
flying lonely above the ruins,
the slight debris of all the fires
I had lived with, wholly consumed by.
All my dust was gone for good,
and that part of me, the breath of God,
glowed without burning, shone with dark light,
danced like fountains at the weightless peak
of pure delight and fell. . . .

I woke up gnashing my teeth.
—Is anything wrong? they asked.
—Did you have a bad dream?
—Do you have a fever?

—I have had a dream of purity, I said.
And then they all laughed
and my mouth stretched with laughter too,
red and white, obscene,
and my tongue was as sweet as a fresh plum again.
And I . . . I was on fire as before.

I have known other dreams,
the ordinary ones:
Myself naked,

riding bareback on a horse
across a country like the moon.
Something is chasing us
(or *me* anyway)
and my little whip sings
and the horse gnaws at the bit.
The wind is like ice water.
Then suddenly the horse is riding me!
I wake up screaming my name.

Another:
Myself with feathers and wings.
But I can't fly. I am caught.
They start to pluck me.
Now each feather is a single hair
yanked by the tender roots.
I try to cry but no sound comes.
My mouth is full of fur.
I wake up and find
I have fallen out of my cold bed.

I tell you all this
not for the pennies of your pity.
Save those coins to cover your eyes.
Nor for your eyebrows
to chevron my rank of shame.
Nor for you to whisper about me
behind your cupped palms.
But that you may know
what a thing it is to be chosen.

I had every right to love and hate holiness.

—What is flesh? you ask.
I have been called sweet,
a hive of dark honey,
worthy of worship
from roots of hair to toes.

And I have been called cruel,
the tormenter of dreams,
a dancer of the abstract fancy.
All of which is a lie.
The plain truth is
I was a creature that sweats,
excretes, sags, ages, wrinkles. . . .
My bones were weary of me.

The soul then?
I think I dreamed it once.

—And the other dreams?
They weren't me. Not me! Not me!
I was not the one who was dreaming.

Bring on the wild man,
bearded like black sky before a storm,
eyes all alight like white water,
wrapped in rags,
skin and bones corrupted by neglect,
a mouth of ruined teeth and bitter breath,
a cripple cursing every dancer.

—How have you come from my dream?
I wanted to say. —Bless me!
I longed to kiss
but my lips spat for me.

Understand this:
I loved him as myself.
God must love His creatures so.

But I was caged.
My skin and bones hated me.
My thoughts hooded me like a wild bird.

The Dance?
Believe what you care to.
Picture it any way you want to.
All the world knows
truth is best revealed
by gradual deception.

My tongue cried for his head.
But it was my mouth that kissed him
and was damned.

Then I was free and able to rejoice.
A bad marriage from the beginning.
Flesh and spirit wrestle
and we call it love.

We couple like dogs in heat.
We shudder and are sundered.
We pursue ourselves,
sniffing, nose to tail
a comic parade of appetites.

That is the truth,
but not the whole truth.
Do me a little justice.
I had a dream of purity
And I have lived in the desert ever since.

The dry branch of a birch tree
beats on my window in whirling Moscow.
At night Siberia sets free a shining wind
against the cold glass. The wind plays
tunes on my fretted nerves, in my mind.
I am sick. Can die from one minute to the next.
I go with you, Varvara Alexandrovna,
making the rounds in little felt shoes
with your quick eyes, nurse of my chances.
I am not afraid of death,
just as I have never feared life.
I think someone else is lying here.
Perhaps, if I can forget love and pity,
the grinding earth and the pale sound
of solitude, I can let go of life.
In the dark your hands burn me, Varvara
Alexandrovna. You have the fingers of my mother
pressing hard to leave the long peace
after pain. You are the human Russia
of the times of Tolstoy and Mayakovsky.
You are Russia; not this country of snow
captured now in a hospital mirror.
You are a multitude of hands reaching for others.

We wandered in a half-lit chilly dark.

Half-lit because the light was sieved
through chinks and cracks and holes.
Chilly because it was already winter.
The tombs, in fact, were closed;
But *lire* seem to be the magic key
to anything this side of heaven's gate.

We stumbled in a half-lit chilly dark
and saw their implements,
(symbolic, of course and nothing like
Egyptian ones you've heard about,
real ships, real swords, real beds)
carved into the living rock.
And we saw their frescoes too,
the sad, wide-eyed, two-dimensional people
we could scarcely believe in,
but there they were, their dark eyes answering
no questions, telling no secrets at all.
There are times when even lovers share this look.

We move into another chamber
where someone giggled.

"Well, they knew how to live,"
our host and guide, a Philadelphian,
Harvard- and museum-trained, said.

What glowed on the walls was *erotica,*
the daydreams and the night thoughts,
the pinned-up wishes of the ancients.
One in particular caught our eyes,
(the light fell on it best).
A slave on all fours in the lady's couch,
and she, thus mounted, lies
back, knees high, to receive
("receive," I believe is the word we use

nowadays, the proper euphemism)
a standing lover
whom nature or art has hugely gifted.
She is no more of flesh and blood
than a playing-card queen,
but still her false face is alive with joy.
She seems to like her shaky perch.
Her lover is much more solemn and intent,
gripping his mighty instrument.
The slave is stolid in his pose.
What is he thinking? God knows.

And we, the creatures of another culture,
one whose truth is seldom in the nude,
whose tombs are plots of silence
and whose dreams are fugitive as spies,
to be caught and shot at first light?
Someone had giggled, somebody joked,
and now in separate privacy we creep
into a crazy house of mirrors
where the self, disguised, assumes
a shiver of swift lewd poses
like the gambler's shuffled deck.

Does it seem strange to go to the dead
for the facts of life?
Orpheus, Virgil, Dante, Christ
descended in the dark and stirred
the troubled bones. And we,
with all hell in our heads,
must follow or go mad.
"Love, let us be true . . . ,"
Old Matthew Arnold sang,
who couldn't have meant what he said.
Or maybe he did. . . .
I have seen a Victorian gentleman's
boot-remover made of brass—

a naked woman whose spread legs
catch and pull off the boot.

We move along and pretty soon
are outside in the open air again.

"Places like this have the kind of truth
that the public monuments conceal,"
an archeologist says.
"Boy, I wouldn't want to be that slave,"
the shy sociologist tells me.

But what I like best is
the classicist from Vassar.
She's suddenly bright-eyed and wordy
like somebody with a fever.
"Until I went down in these tombs
I never really *believed* in ancient times."
She babbles of bones and artifacts
(meanwhile avoids the subject of
the tomb assigned to human love)
and bounces like a little girl
on the back seat all the way home.

Rugby Road

In memory of Hyam Plutzik

1.

My days, these days, begin on a road called Rugby,
a rich name coining counterfeit ivy and distant towers
and the loud cries of far-off playing fields
where all the young men, being English,
belabor each other in impeccable English
while swans go by like a snowy procession of Popes.

O far from Rugby Road!
Far too from all the sweat and blood,
the grunt and groan and scrimmage of a burly game.

My days begin on Rugby Road
where first light blesses everything
with promises not a living soul will keep.

Now I walk past lawns and houses.
And I in turn am passed
            by station wagons,
each awiggle with its cargo of kids,
each one driven by the same housewife.
She wears a formal painted mask
somewhere between the expressions
of comedy and tragedy.

Ah, lady, I have seen
your nightgown dancing
on the clothesline round with wind.
I have danced with your empty nightgown.
I have hoisted it for my sail
and voyaged like a pirate far and wide,
a fool on the Ship of Fools.
I publish no secrets because
I know only my own.

Now stands above an intricate corner
Mr. Jefferson's splendid imitation of
the Pantheon, here called the Rotunda
and used (an old joke goes)
exclusively for a Rotunda.
I walk through the stain of that shadow
and down the colonnade of Mr. Jefferson's Lawn
and finally meet Mr. Jefferson himself,
seated, wearing a pensive, studious look,
expensive eighteenth-century clothes,
and an excellent patina.

Beneath his gaze, boys in coats and ties
go to and from classes, carrying books,
the weight of all our wisdom in their hands.

I think of Jefferson, the eccentric,
dabbler, gadgeteer and dilettante,
high in his crazy castle, Monticello,
which time has also dignified.

A radical who rocked the boat,
who dumped King George and all his tea
into the neutral and indifferent sea.

A virtuoso who could turn
pomp and circumstance into a circus tune.
Who tamed and whipped the lion through hoops of fire.

Time which will tame us one and all,
which can turn love songs into howls,
may yet make music of my groans
or teach me how to sit up and to beg.

2.

I am thinking today of the death of a friend,
a poet, a scholar and a Jew
from whom a Christian gentleman could learn
some charity. I have the news today
that he is dead. "He was in great pain,
but brave until the very last
when his mind wandered."

Where does the mind wander?

Do we go all naked and alone
when flesh and worn-out senses fail?
Or are we at last tailored in radiance,
wearing smiles like an absolute shoeshine?

I dream a playing field, all green and Greek,
where plump, conventional nymphs and satyrs roam
and romp with only sunlight for clothing.
(O far from Rugby Road!)

But you, I believe, have found at last
a ruined wall in a dusty place
and kneel there praying for us now.
I would join you if I dared.

Your prayers are only songs.
These songs become birds and fly
over the wall and into a sudden garden
where trees are dreaming and fountains play
a bloodless, sweatless game of light and air.

And there one day a bird will sing your name
and fountains begin to dance to that new tune
like young girls veiled in moonbeams.

That shade is far too subtle for my mind.
I do not want to die. I fear
my flesh will make me scream before
it lets me wander where I will.

Better to be a bronze imposter.
Better to wear a coat and tie
and babble of green Greek fields.
Better to hold wisdom in one hand.

I fear I can never make the old stones sing.
I fear to leave my flesh and bones behind.
I have forgotten how to say my prayers.

3.

In the halls my colleagues hurry
to classes, conferences, coffee,
all to the tune of ringing bells.
Bells toll to celebrate beginning and the end
of every fifty-minute session where
we deal out knowledge like a pack of cards.
Perhaps we should wear a cap and bells,
belled mortarboards in honor of
a perilous, ridiculous vocation.

there are no bells in that garden
and the leaves of the trees are laughter

We fear the ridiculous more
than a cage full of lions and tigers.

How can the mind begin to wander free
until at last the last pride of the flesh
falls away like a sad fig leaf?

Leaves are falling here and now
to be raked and turned to smoke.

your fountains are vague as the smoke
and the leaves of the trees are laughter
and the birds in the leaves are songs
and the fruit of the trees is sweet
and good to eat

Here in a hall the typewriters chatter,
crickets calling in the language of crickets.
And here the unwandering mortal mind
leaps like a grasshopper, tense and agile,
from one blade of grass to another
on the barbered space we call The Lawn.

Some of us are gathering grapes from thistles
and some are busy baking stones for bread.
Our elders doze and yawn like sheiks,
propped on the pillows of reputation.
"Sir, have you seen Susanna lately?
In secret places have you seen
Wisdom, Sapientia, pale Diana,
white and bare as the winter moon?"
They wink and will not answer.

The young lions roar and jump through hoops.
There is a game like rugby going on,
grunts and groans in impeccable English.

4.

I envy your open weather, Mr. Jefferson,
the rain and shine, the simple pleasure of
a uniform of painless bronze.
Your words endure in marble places.

I honor you, my dead and buried friend,
whose words exist in slender volumes.

Behind the words the song and dance is free,
free as the birds to fly south from the snow.
South to islands, the richest islands,
where our suntans will be tuxedos,
where girls the color of milk and honey
dance and the breeze is French perfume
and the surf is orchids and ermine
and roughest blanket is moonlight.

A bell sounds like a bugle.
I must try to muster my wandering mind.

They are burning up the leaves.
They are burning up the typewriters.
They are folding up their silken tents.

I light a cigarette and reach for a book.
I straighten my tie and grit my teeth
in what I hope and trust will pass
for a polite, uncertain grin.

(Charlottesville, 1962)

1.

Painting Ann-Margret's
my idea of fun
a sopping wet rainbow
of colors that run
a slithery sloppy
a flowery thing
is pretty Ann-Margret
all wrapped in a ring
of slaphappy shades
and pigments quite motley
no wonder gay blades
pursue her so hotly
till she rolls on the canvas
like a pure artifact
it's kind of a pity
Ann-Margret can't act.

2.

Twiggy is leggy and terribly thin
a bustling business & a live mannequin
hustling hairstyles & fashions & maybe a shoe
O living with Twiggy would be living in sin
with a real corporation that's limited too.

Some Twiggys are wooden & found in the store
in long-legged poses in clothes & the nude
and that kind of Twiggy will never be lewd
no matter how shrewdly a man might implore.

O would she or wouldn't she woodenly wantonly
though skinny give any & than many give more
then doze in a dream & brazenly snore?
Alas the bare truth is Twiggy's a bore.

3.

Kim Novak is blonder
than Mother and me
Kim Novak is blonder
than a mother should be

she's blond at the bottom
and all blond on top
O no one in Sodom
was blonder than she

Erotic Norwegians and neurotic Swedes
exposed and uncovered with unseemly speed
will blush like brunettes and world will discover
she's blonder than they and blonder all over
it's Kim Novak's secret and she never tells
why she's blonder and blander than anyone else.

4.

How does it feel to be Barbara Steele,
your face on the screen, your name on a book?
Does it feel quite unreal to be Barbara Steele
like a cake in the mind of a cook?

Is it fun when you peel Miss Barbara Steele?
Does she jump for her life like a trout in a brook?
Does she fall in a trance or suddenly squeal?
Does she dance at the end of a hook?

I feel in my bones that Barbara Steele
would not like this free liberty took,
and like other girls (half sugar, half seal)
never leaps without more than a look.

5.

Donna Michelle
is round as a bell.

Sing hey nonny ninny
    tit willow to woo
Sing hey ninny nonny
    ding dong & ding dong

She's round and she's firm
and wears a suntan
the color of honey
right out of the jar
she's a round and a firm
and a tough-looking honey
to touch her I venture
costs plenty of money.

Sing hey nonny ninny
    sing horny sing ho

She can stand on her head
she can dance like a doll
she can pose on a bed
like Eve before Fall.

Sing Adam and Eve
    and a fig leaf or two

And round goes the world
and round goes the sun
so ring out wild bells
for Donna is one
girl whose roundness
I'm happy to tell

is as sound and as clear
and as true as a bell.

Sing hey horny ninny
dong ding and
ding dong

In my study, blinds drawn, alone
with pen and paper and too many books,
I know what happens in my neighborhood
by sounds, by heart. Here comes the milkman,

his tenor engine humming while
the bottles clink a light percussion.
Dogs bark. They start at the other end
of the street until the whole block is a fugue

of snarls. You'd think it was Judgment Day
the way they carry on to greet
the garbage man, laundry man, postman
walking slowly with his little weight

of dooms. That's best of all,
the progress of the postman. I go
with him, sweating, shifting the bag
as I hand over joy or tribulation

or nothing at all, something or other
addressed to the Occupant. He brings bills.
He gives away pleas, rejections, recriminations.
Love and death lie lightly in his hands.

In my study, blinds drawn, alone
with the rhythm of my pulse and the song
of a trapped fly on the window pane,
I write a postcard he can take away:

"Dear World, Though I have loved you
and lost you, times beyond counting,
still I write upon this instant in receipt
of all your ordinary music to inform you

"that I can't live without you.
I intend, by God, hell and high water,
sleet or snow and the wheel of fortune,
to come back for more of the same.

"I am alone too much with too many books,
with blank paper and my fountain pen.
But enough of that for now. In closing
I send you love and kisses.

"When next I appear, blinking, bear from a cave,
I will tell shocking secrets. Turn on
all your power mowers. I'll drown them out.
Let every dog bark! I remain yours truly."

1.

Cheerleader
Bouncer of basketballs
Stern keeper of homeplate
She ran on beautiful strong legs
around my dreams for a full year
bright hair streaming behind her
and laughter like golden apples
daring one and all to muster
energy to master her

I am sorry
I was not the one.

2.

She was a hearty
    country girl
blonder than peaches & sturdy
    as a Percheron
could climb trees like a squirrel
    & plow like a grown man
& laugh like an acrobatic angel
    in all weathers

Once we lay down on the sweet grass
    in a cool shade
leaves dancing to their own whispers
& a bluejay scolding both of us
    with a woodwind tune

—Don't leave your coat and hat, she said,
'cause we won't be coming back this way.

3.

Sensitive
she moved easy to tears
for example by

sunset woodsmoke seashells kittens
poetry from The Romantic Movement

I see her yet in a wide hat veiled
swan-graceful in our canoe
cool fingers coaxing a guitar

I can hear her singing *Greensleeves*
Barbara Allen & *Go Away from My Window*
& always *The Golden Vanitie*

And when I sank her in the lowlands O
she laughed louder than the 3 witches
she gnashed her teeth & cried out
a foreign legion of four-letter words
      like little prayers

4.

Remember how we went to church together,
from thence to the Palm Court of the Plaza
where we drank milk punch and tried to talk
theology (of all things!), joy and suffering?

Will your wide eyes brighten now
and what will your eyebrows ever do
if I stop fooling long enough
to tell the truth? Tell the truth
in love, St. Paul said. I would not
hurt you with a lie to lie with you.

I would, however, I confess,
cheerfully, gently undress you altogether
and, equally cheerful, gentle as can be,
hold tight to altogether while we fell
down breathless miles of waterfall
and rock-and-roll of roller coaster rides.

Into your circus tent I'd creep
without a ticket stub or conscience
to spank my palms in loud applause
for the shining bareback rider.

Your smile is worth waking for.
The ample pleasures of your city
(o whiter than Paris) worth a Mass.

I here confess I suffered that Palm Sunday,
a stylite burning painless in the Plaza
where words like buzzards soared and sailed.

I think you are made of milk and honey.
I live in a desert of hot rocks.

O Lord, here I hang by bad jokes,
like thumbs, just to make her laugh.
Will she pray for me next time she's kneeling,
light candles, wear a birthday suit?

Listen, to make your clear eyes brighten
and widen with waking wonder, I
shake hands with suffering and rejoice.
I will bear witness in the unknown tongue
though every theologian crow and though
your eyebrows rise higher than hawks.

5.
Why do I sing and celebrate the mad wild girl?

She whose long hair was dark and live as snakes.
Her eyes were brilliant hard and lost
like agates on the playground of the spring.
Laughter sudden and mysterious and coarse
as a cat's tongue. Oh and her body was bow
without an arrow, a lute without one string.

Loving was always to wrestle in the dark
with later sobs and a rustle of chilly sheets.

Where are you going? I called from the shore.
My answer was in salt and sting of wind.
She sailed close to the wind, heeled and vanished.

I could not heal her. I swear that no man could.
I think one day she'll learn to grin all right,
when she's a painted doll calm in a satin coffin.

To make the best of it, I cried *Bon voyage!*
Hiked and shrugged my shoulders like a soldier's pack
and went off like a bumblebee to girls like flowers
who smile and sway in veils of common sun and rain.

She drank straight wormwood, cut her teeth on bark.
Frantic she ran from packs of yaps and snarls.
And in her dreams she was a willow tree.

Let the wild dogs take her then.
Let her bones rest in lonely peace.
I'll find another piece of milk and honey,
sweet milk, dark honey, bread and wine.
I'll pick up all my marbles and go home.

Why do I wake now in the middle of a dream
to smoke and pace and curse her Christian name?
Why shiver again for kisses ghostly cold,
shudder at skulls, all tongueless, bald . . . ?
I pinch to see if I have turned to stone.

She never even said goodbye to me,
whose heart lies broken at the bottom of the sea.

6.

Silence is darkly plural.
Sounds and noises die at once.
I listen to them fade and go.

I have known many silences,
of midnight, high noon, of dawn,
then the scream of a saw, cry of an ax,
or the least breath of breeze in the dusty leaves
might have been purest music.

I have heard the bright new songs
of birds and buds proclaiming spring
and the drunken hum of swarming bees
and the drumtaps of my marching heart. . . .

I have longed for perfect silence
with a truly bitter thirst.

Frost in my veins and nerves,
dying in bits and pieces,
I doze and dream like a lazy snake.

Your sudden music batters, breaks the spell.
I open my eyes and see you dance like water,
sweet water, fresh water, light dazzled, poured
over edge of lip and rim to flash in a rush
and shatter like glass in the sun.

And now you bathe in a shower of old gold.
I wake to the joy of a new song and dance
I never dreamed of in clamor or quiet.

I blink, I stretch, uncoil and rejoice,
o bright and wholly singular girl!

Be still my broken bones.
Be still for as long as she dances.
Let me listen and be silent.

If ever she would falter and fall,
I will kiss her awake with all my wounds
and clang a fine tune on my chains.

7.

Wahoo! Wee-doggie! Let me die this way!
She cried aloud at the top of her voice.
It was, of course, our very first time,
and the first is always the best, they say.

But soon she was in a different mood
when she sat fully dressed on the bed.
I assure you it was all a dream, she said.
And I: *I only dreamed you in the nude.*

(after the French of Paul-Jean Toulet)

8.

girl in a black raincoat

sing about her here & now not later

there are always some things
better not recollected in tranquility

who never a daffodil could dance
nor even like the poorest grass
all o watered with sweat & tears
fed with sweet marrow of dry bones
cut clipped rolled & edged
can sway to the whims of the breeze

yet she did dance a little while
ah & her least whim or glance
could wake from cold heart more joy
than cascades of silver dollars
from finest slot machines

so let her gambol while I still gamble
betting it all on life love light

while the old dealer in a pair of dark glasses
shuffles to palm the ace of spades

see her dance to the edge of the world
& look down though warned against it
to count stars & see them glitter & shiver
Goodbye! She cries & chooses
doffing darkness & flashing head over heels
brightness forever as she takes the long fall
        See you later . . . !

goodbye girl
I lose you lose he she it loses
though death's the old man who shuffles & deals
yet will grass grow & daffodils will dance
and be resurrected in tranquility
o she's long gone &
I pause to praise her here & now

9.
She is so beautiful in the morning.

She wakes from her dream like a bird,
a ghost of the dew and the cold.
Yawns then and opens eyes
the color of cloudless skies.
Smiles brighter than new pennies.
Laughs like little bells in light wind.

Face to face with her amazing dawn,
who will deny my civil rights
to stamp my hooves like a snaredrum?
Who says I can't salute
when the rooster of my thighs
cries *cockadoodledoo?*

10.

When all our songs, both yours and mine,
die with breath to drown in dust,
will feet of unborn children rock and roll
like thunder over our thin roof of earth?

Well, what's in a name or a song
when the sun is only shining
and the wind is rife with seeds?

Dust is dancing in a waterfall of light,
see, now! through my window panes.
We read your poems and talk around them.
They are writing love poems for you,
as is meet and right to do, and I,
I look toward light and see a dance of dust.

So every song and dance must end and then
begin again. Another throat and other lips,
hair like honey and eyes more brightly blue
than the breezy, kite-crazy skies of early March. . . .

Come what April and let my skull grin.
I too have danced as I swivel now
in my teacher's swivel chair like a toy.
You sip your milkshake through a straw.
I believe the world is sweeter than they say.

11.

A bright and clever poet
has not only written but published
a poem about my wife.

He celebrates
the formal calm and grace
she wears like a magic cloak
when she coins the golden notes
of Bach, Frescobaldi, Dowland,
spinning only the purest sound
from her fine Velasquez guitar.

Clearly this is a poem
I should have written.

Oh never doubt it for one minute
I have dreamed a poem for you
a thousand times and a thousand times
have tested my skill and failed.

Now I am only green envy.
My fingers are ten fat thumbs.

How will I ever write a poem for you?

You who are all my music,
whose dancing is the only dance I know,
whose eyes and smile make all my light.

You whom I choose and hold
in dream and nightmare, fire and flood,
ever and always in flesh and blood.

You whom I would choose to praise
though all guitars were kindling wood
and every clever poet were mute.

12.

Having tested & tasted
your fine flesh will all 5
clumsy eager hungry senses
(though lightly gently slightly)
I am now more than 5 mouths

O I taste & touch the savor
of 7 seas & the burning sun
and (just there) the cool light
of a new moon & the old song
of long & lonesome journey

Now I may believe in the world
I think the world may be round
and firm & free & easy to love
I rejoice in all your round worlds
I know where you are silk & spice

7 seas to cross & 7 gates too
to conquer a tall castle
Lance & spur & sword I ride
amid roses & barbwire of briars
to kiss you while you dream

Sweet dreamer o my slow smiler
if you wake not if lost & tossed
I sail right over the edge of flat earth
consider this Until I sleep for good
my 5 & foolish grins are only yours.

13.

Warm sun and sweet wind
new leaves greener than memory
dogwood more delicate than brides
tulips lax as after love

Warm sun and sweet wind

I lie in the sun to think
I think that I might be happy
if you came to me here and now
wearing sunlight o sweeter than wind

I lie here drunk with dreaming you
Come to me now and I will cover
completely you with a robe of kisses
Be still as a flower while I whisper

my secrets to your secret places

Instead of a Love Poem

There's no sense in any of it
paper envelopes and postage stamps

neither for love nor money
and why else would a sane man

not even for a pat on the back
from our Pres-i-dent
not one jillion pairs of palms
pink and glowing with applause
would be worth it

would be worth
my hand and yours
your pink and mine
or any of your glowing

I pat you and I make
my own applause

so
lie back easy love
let stars in your eyes
be our only light
here now and always

you can trust me
not a word of this
no jot or tittle
no least whisper to repeat
in verse or prose

I'll keep our secret secret
and save a postage stamp

Same Old Story

I will be dead
and you will be dead.
It's a natural fact.

If I start to shiver
may I warm my hands
by your white fire?

Listen, snowmaiden,
my sleeping princess, while
I begin to shimmy and shake
and make a kind of lonesome dance
with the rattle and jangle of bones.

The maestro approaches the podium.

What you fear most of all
is not the inevitable custard pie
nor banana peels and whoopie cushions
nor even the raucous laughter of
the dark gods of your dreams.
I think you fear that one bright wink
will signal your shame to the world.

Turns and bows to the audience.

I never saw anyone grin
back at a grinning skull.
Did you?
Why be proud and lonely?
Trust me.
If you ever catch cold
let me be your boyscout
with my miracle of matchless fire.

Come let us wink together
and laugh in the light and the dark.

You say why.
I say why not.
O tedious dialectic!
I know a dance for two.

The maestro raises his baton.

Three Short Ones

(1) definition

What we spend first of all is innocence
which, after all, we never owned,
but like a borrowed book returned
unread, or like a secret was not kept
but published though the whole world wept.

(2) an epigram by Martial

To the reader: when you look
inside, you're bound to find here
some good verses, some middling, and I fear
plenty of bad ones. What can I say?
Buddy, it's the only way
a poet can make a book.

(3) little tune

The rent payment's due. Got holes in my shoes.
The world turned upside down. I read it in the *News*.
The color of a sigh is the color of the blues.

Shards for Her

You are the spirit dancing in seven veils.
(I watch you from my bed of nails.)

You know the deep places of the sea.
You know the dance of fountains in the light.
You are the spirit dancing in seven veils.

You breathe the keen air of mountains.
You have seen the glare of heatstricken, silent places.
(I see you from my bed of nails.)

You bring me the green heart of springtime.
I taste. It is bitter and good.
You are the spirit dancing in seven veils.

You are all my light
when I wrestle with angels and daemons.
Come, love me on a bed of nails.

Manifesto

For R. H. W. Dillard

to begin again

after a long time
and many promises
not to say anything
not to add another voice
to the damned cacophony
cacophony of the damned
makers of verses
spinning prayerwheels
of speculation & gossip
fast & faster
till words are gone
all voices howl & moan
becoming at last
the humming tune
of a whirling top

o prayerwheels & tops
who is able
to translate you

who reads you
loud & clear

avoid poets
as once ancestors
carefully avoided
lepers with little bells

evade eloquence
a beggar's palm
hungry for coins

elude logic
a clenched fist
to break noses

how many times
facing a waste
of blank paper
have I said
nothing no not one
not one least leaf
falling to flame or
flagging the spring's
first & final heat
not one southward
surge of birds
nor even the song
of their returning
not laughter & tears
neither body dreaming
nor mind gambling
nor spirit kneeling. . . .

No swore I no nothing
under the sun & moon
will make me begin again

who has wrestled angels
feeling flesh wither
who has danced with demons
drunk on all fours
knows what I mean

who for all honor
have yet said
instead of keeping
holy silence
have left unsaid
when words were kisses
know I mean well

who too much has seen
of naked untruth
too often heard
the old songs pass
like dirty pennies
from palm to palm
he reads me
loud & clear

yet have I today
shameless gone forth

o damned cacophony
what have I done

confess
I bought a notebook
and a new fountain pen

to begin again
ring little bells
to begin

The pen is red.

From

Welcome to the Medicine Show

(1978)

Since It Is Valentine's Day

Nothing but trouble from now on (you said),
a rawhide string of Februaries.

My stomach growls agreement.
I have arrived at the age of half-truths.

Since it is Valentine's Day, I can remember
bodies and beds, the breath and the flesh

of others, each one a perfect stranger now.
I have lost their names like marbles on the schoolyard.

For better or worse, in sickness and in health,
self-incrimination replaces self-delusion.

I count your sum of scars and subtract my own.

Your eyes, brighter and bluer than many,
are more like eloquence and sorrow.

Try as I will, when we touch,
I shrug old bones and cut my losses

into the shapes of stars, of hearts and flowers.
When you say doom, I hear a blooming rose.

Body be laughter . . .

My horseless carriage
my old engine
stutters and dies
a lemon off the lot

Quit stalling
Go tell her right now
how her eyes and what her walk
how much darker her hair than
and whitest her bare back must be

Tell her that
twin fine horses prance
her admirably magic coach
directly to the prince's dance
Say her voice
is like clarinets
all dark ebony and silver

Body is laughter . . .

What chance
has he got whose heart
is a toy drum
whose music is made
by a tin whistle
and whose head is
irreparably pumpkin

Too many miles
on the map of my flesh
I cough and stammer
rattle and rumble
and end up standing
by the side of the road

raising a bald thumb
and my very best smile

Home is wherever
you are going
wherever you want to
take me to . . .

"Wisely," she writes, "I have just turned down a date
with a gentleman recently on the cover of *Time* magazine."

Nixon? I wonder. *Ford? Rockerfeller?*
Who else has there been lately? "Jack Nicholson,"

my wife, patient with my enormous ignorance, says
as she bends over the ironingboard. "That's who!"

Too bad, Jack, boy. When she walks into a room,
groins react like the Guards to "God Save the Queen."

She used to work for *Cosmo* and now writes poems.
"Maybe she could have written a poem about it."

"I doubt it," my wife says. "I don't imagine
a fling with Nicholson is exactly a poetic experience."

Color of honey, breasts like Tahiti, more curves
than the road from Roanoke to Grundy, Virginia.

Eyes dark with secrets and bright with promises.
Lips that shine wetly, *just* like a *Cosmo* girl.

Too bad, Jack. She writes poetry and letters
about fine and fancy times in New York City

and all the people, famous, glamorous, notorious,
the celebrities she either goes out with or doesn't.

Too bad, George. You live by a river (far from the city)
where seagulls cry like children lost in the fog.

I believe she is really the goddess Fortuna in disguise,
fickle and faithless, desired and wholly desirable,

like that seashell woman out of deepest ancient dreams
who makes wisdom look like somebody's plain little sister.

"I'll never be on the cover of any magazine,"
I say. "I'll never travel to Tahiti or any place like that.

"Dark, beautiful women never write poems about me.
Guess I'll never have any luck or magic again!"

"Tough shit!" my tall and beautiful wife replies,
folding my shirts while the steamiron sighs.

"Why don't you write a poem about that?"
Lucky in love, laughing and scratching, I swear I never will.

To a Certain Critic

Walking in the woods, you turn over a rotten log.
Out from under crawls something very snotlike and pale.
If it could open its mouth and talk good English,
you'd know exactly what you sound like to me.

Another Literary Wife

"All I ever wanted," this pretty woman tells me,
"was a guy with the body of a truck driver and the soul of a poet.
And look what I got . . . ! Just see for yourself . . .
An Iowa City Mumbler with a build like Archie Bunker."

One of Our More Fashionable Poets

His best-dressed lines all read like the subtitles
of an old foreign movie in black and white.
His enigmatic metaphors tend mostly to sound
like illegal aliens learning Basic English.

To a Rival Poet

Lights out in the barracks and always then
a hallelujah chorus of farts commenced,
the least of which was more like music
and sweeter, too, than any two of yours.

Book Review

I am using your pages
to start wet kindling wood.
Amazing such pale poems
can make a bright fire!

Introduction to Contemporary Literary Criticism

What Professor Helen Vendler actually said
(in Boston on January 18th, 1978):
"If she had only been able to keep her health,
Flannery O'Connor might have made it in New York."

Portrait of the Artist as a Cartoon
Silence, exile, cunning, I resolve to embrace
them gladly, proudly; and then the phone rings
and I trip and fall all over myself
running for it, hoping it's for me,
praying my luck has changed, my time has come.

I Must Have Peaked Too Early
"Sir, Madame, Person, Occupant,"
the National Endowment addresses me.
"There's still space available and plenty of time
to reserve some of the same for your mortal remains
at the Tomb of the Unknown American Writer."

Welcome to the Medicine Show
What I have done here is simply to bottle
some of the natural hatred and malice of poets for each other.
I guarantee it will do nothing at all for you.
But it will sure enough shame a hornet or a scorpion.
It can make a rattlesnake laugh and roll over like a puppy dog.

My Main Confessional Poem
I confess
I am not guilty
of anything I'd care
to tell you about.

Worldly Wisdom on My Forty-Eighth Birthday
True, I'll never be rich or famous or beautiful.
But today I still have the good sense to invite you
to come a little closer and kiss my bare knuckles.
Try to ride on my kneecap like a rodeo bronco.

Lunatic Song

Under the stark naked moon
    I sing one note
Give me the proper tool
so I can cut my throat

Consolation of Philosophy

for Maria Katzenbach

Art is long
and I am short.

My Grand Strategy

There ain't no good
in a wornout broom
Going to get me a brand new one
and sweep out my living room

End of April

Do I really need to tell you
how suddenly light my body becomes
when fallen cherry blossoms smear
sweetness all over my shoes?

Late Night Rain

Tonight only a timid pest
sprinting away across my dark lawn
like the last drunken guest.

Splitting Wood

Feet apart ax at arm's length over head
I swing downhard now and easy
falls open a whole length of oak log
freeing the white sweet brief ghostly fragrance
Which is really something
    may be every thing

Same Old Story
My dancing girls are here to stay.
Though whipped and chased away
like money changers, they
always set up shop again
to take away my takehome pay.

Let It Be Our Little Secret
All too true that your face
is turning to leathery lines,
but oh-me-and-oh-my the rest
of you shines like newborn.

Since You Asked Me, I Guess I'd Better Tell You
A perfectly thrilling intensity which can only be achieved
        by total freedom from the boring burden of character,

and this closely coupled with the almost complete absence of
        even the basic, most commonplace of virtues and values,

and all of the above linked together with the explicit and
        continual presence of her irremediable selfishness,

these are the obvious lures that light up a man in the same way
        as flame does the wings of a hairy moth.

Jacob
Years and scars later
I finally learn
all angels travel
under assumed names.

Easter
Lord, in your light rising,
pray lift my heavy spirit, too.

She writes him at his home address:
"What I mainly want to do
is fuck you in front of your wife.
I'd like to make it in the presence of
all the women you've been to bed with.
I want to do it before an audience composed
of every woman you have ever known!"

He frames a reply with care:
"Naturally I understand the nature of your feelings
and appreciate your rare sincerity and candor,
but believe me when I say I'm not at all sure
these things form the ideal foundation for
a viable student-teacher relationship."

Snapshot: Italian Lesson

When I hear of the death of a major poet these days,
I remember Rome, 1958, myself standing alongside an
    enormous priest
by a newspaper kiosk in Trastevere, staring at headlines—
IL PAPA E MORTO! As the priest turns away a voice from
    the crowd
(all too poor to buy a paper) calls out: "Is it true the Holy Father
    is dead?"
The priest nods, then shrugs hugely and answers in the local dialect:
"Better him than us, eh? Better him than us." And walks off to
    his chores
among the poor who are always with us even until the end of
    the world.

From

Luck's Shining Child

(1981)

Because I am broke again
I have the soles of my shoes repaired
one at a time.

From now on one will always be
fat and slick with new leather
while his sad twin,

lean and thin as a fallen leaf,
will hug a large hole like a wound.
When it rains

one sock and one foot get wet.
When I cross the gravel parking lot
one foot winces

and I have to hop along on the other.
My students believe I am trying
to prove something.

They think I'm being a symbol of
dichotomy, duality, double-dealing,
yin and yang.

I am hopping because it hurts.
Because there is a hole in my shoe.
Because I feel poor for keeps.

What I am trying not to do
is imagine how it will be in my coffin,
heels down, soles up,

all rouged and grinning above my polished shoes,
one or the other a respectable brother
and one or the other

that wild prodigal whom I love
as much or more than his sleek companion,
luck's shining child.

Leaving the cocktail party
I steal the Admiral's hat
At home I try it on
See how much it changes me

Now I am purely different
I am handsome I am jaunty
I have pride and power on my head

Let him be sad and ashamed
Let him curse himself and whoever took it
Let him feel hopeless and lost without it
Let his wife laugh in his naked face

Listen Admiral it fits me fine
It looks just right on my closet shelf
My family will preserve it in my memory
My future history will be worthy of it

Sir I thank you kindly for it
And I solemnly promise never to stand
downcast and shifty in front of anyone
with your hat humble in my hands

Familiar Riddle

What month is this
older than February
greener than envy and money
rich with dark winds
and sudden cloudless thunder?

What day is this
slower than Monday
breathless and completely empty
of birdsongs and sirens
while crowds swarm everywhere?

What age is this
brighter than the Renaissance
and brutal in arts and crafts
abundantly harvesting
tall silos of gold teeth?

What creature is
this stranger beside me
naked and calm as a corpse
yet breathing and speaking
my secrets from a dream?

What child is this
wounded and smiling
armed with a new shiny knife
and flowers for an early grave
who wears my face like his own?

Gone then the chipped demitasse cups
at dawn, rich with fresh cream and coffee,
a fire on the hearth, winter and summer,
a silk dandy's bathrobe, the black Havana cigar.

Gone the pet turkey gobbler, the dogs and geese,
a yard full of chickens feeling the shadow of a hawk,
the tall barn with cows and a plough horse, with corn,
with hay spilling out of the loft, festooning the dead Pierce Arrow.

Gone the chipped oak sideboards and table,
heavy with aplenty of dented, dusty silverware.
Gone the service pistol and the elephant rifle
and the great bland moosehead on the wall.

"Two things," you told me once, "will keep
the democratic spirit of this country alive—
the free public schools and the petit jury."
Both of these things are going, too, now, Grandfather.

You had five sons and three daughters,
and they are all dead or dying slow and sure.
Even the grandchildren are riddled with casualties.
You would not believe these bitter, shiny times.

What became of all our energy and swagger?
At ninety you went out and campaigned for Adlai Stevenson
in South Carolina. And at my age I have to force
myself to vote, choosing among scoundrels.

Dancing Class

On certain days when wind and tide and sun
cease their ancient struggle and begin to dance,
the river runs clear and clean again, and I
would drink from it if I didn't know better.

Today there are birds and yellow butterflies,
bumblebees browsing and humming over clover,
and gulls turning and crying above the river,
riding a light breeze that teases flags and sails.

My eldest son, my firstborn, lies alone in his room,
home from hard failures, wounded, hoping
the sound of loud music will clear his aching head
of shadows and silt, the pale grin of his own grave.

It is folly to drink. The river water is poison.
Hear how the gulls cry out like cats in the night.
After all our wrestling, our sacrificial wounds,
can father and son ever learn to live together?

If I could, I would bring him this day like a glass,
window, or mirror, to look into and through,
if only to see himself wink like an angel
or a perfect stranger worth listening to.

The Roman Catholic bells of Princeton, New Jersey,
wake me from rousing dreams into a resounding hangover.
Sweet Jesus, my life is hateful to me.
Seven a.m. and time to walk my dog on a leash.

Ice on the sidewalk and in the gutters,
and the wind comes down our one-way street
like a deuce-and-a-half, a six-by, a semi,
huge with a cold load of growls.

There's not one leaf left to bear witness,
with twitch and scuttle, rattle and rasp,
against the blatant roaring of the wrongway wind.
Only my nose running and my face frozen

into a kind of a grin which has nothing to do
with the ice and the wind or death and December,
but joy pure and simple when my black and tan puppy,
for the first time ever, lifts his hind leg to pee.

Maine Morning

Where clear air blew off the land,
wind turns around and the sky changes.
Where there was burning blue is pale gray now,
heavy and salty from the cold open sea.
And the long groaning of the foghorn
saying *change . . . change . . . change . . .*
like a sleeper dreaming and breathing.

Tide turning, too, with the weather.
The lobster boats swing about to pull
against moorings like large dogs on chains.
Gulls cry like hurt children and disappear.
And I think, surely it is a magician,
bitter and clever, who has pulled this trick.

That old magician is laughing in the fog.
And the cries of wounded children fade away
while the bellbuoy sounds *farewell . . . farewell . . .*
daring the dead to rise up from dreaming,
to hold their lives like water in their hands.

I wake up to discover
that I am made out of lead again
my feet and hands my toes and fingers
are all poured and moulded
Even my heart clanks dull and heavy

Dull and heavy I clank to the window
and raise the shade on a bluebright river
with tall masts tilting and bobbing in light
and light gulls tilting on a wide seabreeze
crying out their terrible headlines

And all I can imagine is Christopher Columbus
his heart too like a bowling ball
and gulls all around screaming for garbage
being lifted up and easy as a cork on the wave
and seeing then the undeniable green shoreline

Or stout Balboa rusty as an old woodstove
inching his bulky self up to another limb
sweat dripping beneath his dented helmet
then inching his dented helmet above another
whose leaves sigh with his weight and weariness

To see suddenly and always the blue eye of God
which greets his gasp with an enormous wink
The river is burning and the gulls cry doom
but the man of lead now smiles to discover
that even his teeth are rich with silver and gold

Pathetic Fallacy

Gray thoughts   dark laughter   cold words
and we are old enough to know
better than to take this color   this weather
for our very own   and yet we do
just that   greeting a gray wet day
with the wind out of the northeast
riddled with rain   waves like white feathers
flung across the dark tide   the dark river
while drab gulls soar and circle and cry out
the relentless syllables of pure insatiable appetite
we too swallow this morning whole
grow huge with it   heavy with it

Risen shades   thin shadows   coats and layers
of glare ice   frozen slush   patches of old snow
and the wide slack moronic yawning horizon
shabby waste of woodsmoke overflowing   falling
heavy to be lazy scattered by the pale wind
where I'm walking squinting   leaning into it
breathing it deeply in   myself wrapped in rags
of gray thought   talking to myself
myself a yawning stranger   gray on gray

How It Is, How It Was, How It Will Be

How it is
on the next day after
the blizzard
how the sky clears   blues   brightens
cloudless and clean with the old moon
floating here and there quiet and grinning
and the quiet fallen snow
glinting   winking   glittering
(is there one and only word for it?)
with abundance   opulence   extravagance
of (one and only) sunlight
how my breath and the river's
do steam and ghost and shimmyshake
in this purely cold air
how now we know
that we shall surely live forever
how now we want to

A little sun   a light south wind
and all of a sudden we're in the big middle
of mud season   O long time yet before the lilacs
or anything else   even first green leaves
my loud proud black and tan hound dog
stands to bark at a lone crow high in the dead
limbs of the dying elm next door
Crow shrugs   as only crows can
if crows can   he's lonesome up there all alone
I'm richer owning my own hound dog and also
today all that wrinkling of dazzling gold
on the windy river   as well as
all the fresh thick mud my boots can
gorge and carry   Crow he's a whole lot lighter
if poorer   He can shrug and flap
ragged wings to rise out of the branches
Shrug and flap and fly away   black
as my best thought   a piece of burnt paper
one moody poem too muddy to believe

Annual Surrender

Here (again!) an air full of white flakes,
now made only of petals and apple blossoms,
fleeing and falling to lie bright and still
like cast away coats on fields of new grass.

Besieged, we learned to hold our bitter tongues,
to cling to a crumbling dust of nothing
in clenched fists. Nailed up our lean hopes
like shabby hides on all our doors.

Comes now lord sun with trumpets and trombones.
Come trees with green flags, troops of drunken flowers.
Come forth again these blinking thin survivors,
you and I to open fists and flex our fingers.

To pick up shining pieces one more time.

Summer Thunder Storm

for R. H. W. Dillard

Those ancient sisters
who we imagine
imagine they can
decide our destinies
with a shrug and a yawn
with less excitement
among them than
the gentle giggling
with which they greet
routine displays
of common flatulence
sudden and sourceless
among doily and tea cozy
in their dusty living room
those three sisters
have been dropping
knitting needles of rain
whole drawers and trays
full of gold-plated forks
of lightning
our way all day
not to mention
their older brother
somewhere or other
in attic or cellar
an enraged drummer
deranged tympanist
mad as a hatter
and fully responsible for
those howitzers of thunder
whose rolling barrage
has driven my dog
to take cover
in his safest place
behind the sofa

Sisters your needles
have blinded the dark
eyes of our river
your forked lightning
ripped and rent asunder
our sackcloth of sky
and trees pitch and roll
now tossing now jibing
forlorn in the pelt and howl
while my old house
shivers and shakes
and shudders and now
my old dog whimpers
and I   I curse and rejoice
too   finding and keeping
this ordinary emblem
for fury and frustration
while the rain turns into
wild mustangs on my roof
and my feet join in changing
into cossacks and clog dancers
and my howls begin to harmonize
with the wind's in the trees

And so I must dance and howl
though I know well enough
the dust and long sorrows
of your cluttered parlor
though I have often studied
the indecipherable texts
and peered at the pictures
in the fading books there
though I know also
how a blue cool day
lazy and theatrical
is already moving this way
from Canada to make of tomorrow

what it will be   must be
as shining and clear
as white stones in a brook

O believe you me
I know perfectly well
at heart   by heart
how the amazing brightness
is theatrically moving
this way   my way   here and now
to invite me to swallow
my pride and my shame
my fury and frustration
laughing out loud then
when dawn will declare
how my despair and yours
o weary sisters   o witless brother
and even as well the splendid despair
of tragic heroes and kings
will be as if nothing at all
will be remembered if at all
as being purely and only
as brief and foolish
sudden and foolish
after all
as that almost silent noise
which set three sisters giggling

It was, of course,
the dog
who did it.

All night long
sitting alongside
my dead friend
(he with white teeth
gnashed in a grin
at the pale moon
he with stiff hands
reaching for
the darkest zone
of my own silence)
        I have been writing
        love letters.

I have never
felt so much
        alive.

(after the Italian of Giuseppe Ungaretti)

Plough

They planted mines in this field.
On hands and knees, exact, precise,
soldiers laid out row on perfect row.
What kind of crop could it yield?

Chaff. A few thin stacks of the dead.
And left a lone plough in the place
where the farmer vanished in a puff of smoke.
He screamed like a butchered pig, they said.

Home is where they've gone to now,
leaving behind them, calmly waiting for
another pair of hands, another season,
beautiful, see, there stands the plough.

(from the German of Max Barthel)

One time I talked to a goat.
Rain-soaked, stuffed with grass,
she stood all alone in a field,
tied to a post and bleating.

Her cries were the echo of
my inner grief, and I answered,
at first for a joke, but then because
grief is eternal and everywhere speaks
with the same tone of voice. I heard
that voice in the groans of a goat.

From a goat with a face like a Jew
I learned by heart the ancient wail,
the lament of all living things.

(from the Italian of Umberto Saba)

We shall die apart. It is enough
to lie here, pillowed by your palms,
while you study my contour lines
as a chart for future voyages.

We know little enough
about the soul. You may believe
    (under this hollow urn of night)
you sleep in a sweet plantation breeze
spawned by these cold stones . . .

O men and brethren!
Maybe after a thousand such winters
some scholar will make a footnote
for our lonely tomb:

"Nobody chained these lovers
together in a single grave."

(from the Italian of Cristina Campo)

Whore on Crutches in a Bar on Via Della Croce

Once my two legs loved to leap.
Fine twin horses pulled my cart.
Happy awake or fast asleep,
a body of laughter was all my art.
People acted so funny when I clowned around.
They never knew whether to grin or frown.

What's the use of laughing now?
War has improved my basic charms.
Our Liberators taught me how
to walk on crutches without harm.
You ought to see the kind of looks I get.
My stump is the sun in a rumpled sheet.

(from the Italian of Edoardo Cacciatore)

After pleas and persuasion, all the frozen
and uniform gestures of prose,
having said my say, my hup and hip,
the closeorder rhythms of dismounted drill,
I have come back alone to naked verse—
a man singing and dancing in the shower.

God knows I have known the deepest cold,
have slept with snow and waked to wind,
to shining wind blowing all the white way
from old Siberia. We huddled then
by little fires, blew on blue fingers,
called coffee more precious than blood.

Goodbye boots and parka. So long
to the clumsy soupbowl of my helmet.
Pack and rifle, belts and gear all gone,
I hang my dogtags and towel on a nail
to lightheaded, lighthearted, stand
in rosy steam and sing your name

and mine again. O what is a man
singing offkey with pure joy,
dancing loosejointed calypso and highlife,
with no more weight to carry now
than one slight, brightly astonished heart?
Go ask somebody else. I am alive again.

I who was cold to bones am warm and clean.
I who was heavy as a walking bear
am bare of all burdens and briefly free
of fear for now and do not give a damn
who hears my voice and laughs out loud.
Clown or shorn lamb, I have my pride.

But if you happen to laugh, I'll be happy.
And if you choose to clap your hands,
I'll dance until I droop and rise again.
I'll shower you with roses and breathe steam.
I am unarmed. I do not even have a knife.
The letter kills, the spirit giveth life.

Carnival Poem

I see completely through you, lady,
dark lady, though I see darkly.
To travel in the Tunnel of Love
I take your hand and you lead me
to the Funhouse of Mirrors where I
learn by heart your ways and moods.
You make faces while I grow fat and thin,
grotesque, a clown beside your curves.
Faced with so many, how can I choose one?

Round go the rides and the merry-go-round,
clad in lights and laughter and music.
We blow smoke rings at each other.
Frog, fish, bird, who am I now?
Priestess, princess, forest nymph,
dancer or dreamer, which do I dare
to touch? And if we move to kiss,
which one will turn from that to stone?
Will you vanish like the Witch of the North?

Mouthful of cotton candy sweetness,
armsful of highpriced, hardearned dolls,
cradling that tawdry brood of children
not your own, you do not answer me.
When I walk through mirrors, I enter green
fields in a sudden garden of stained glass
where you are dressed in only sunlight.
And I name you Eve. Come take my hand.
Kiss me and I may yet prove to be a prince.

Apology

Berryman wrote sonnets and published them, too,
to tell it all, to tell it all like Petrarch.
And so would I. So would I, except

there's much I do not dare to tell myself
and just as much that I'd tell you and no one else.
And you have secrets that I'll never live to know.

So be it. So be. "So go be," as they say
in the West Indies. Those coffee and chocolate girls
who walk like a lovely ribbon easy unrolling.

Except, too, there's no story here to show and tell.
Light facts fly up and away and cry like gulls,
and the sea leans and tilts with or without them.

So let me confess this much and no more.
You are my Caribbean, salt and sun, richer than China.
You are coffee and chocolate to my taste, your breath

the breeze off distant islands, sweet and strange.
You have secret harbors, and your touch is fever to my flesh.
Your laughter is fresh water. Your kisses are ripe fruit.

Give fame then to all surviving sonneteers.
Sad chains for the few who promised China.
Smile for the man with only bright eyes and a fever.

What can I do but babble this nonsense and report
prodigies which no one else will believe, except
I believe in you always as I believe my own name.

In a bad time
my five senses are
spies in disguise
who say old prayers
undress in the dark
and die at dawn.

It's a bad tune
to march to
while baldest words
wear wigs and pure lies
jangle in fine purses
of pig's ear.

It's a bad dream
where nothing is strange
except what is
only simple.
We live on the kisses
of enemies.

See the bad man
kill with his smile.
He teaches how to dance
at the end of a rope.
Whatever he can kiss
he claims he owns.

O it's a bad time
to make promises
when the words have lost
all salt and savor,
when the finest shining
is on fixed bayonets.

Now's our last chance
for reaching and touching—
to undress bold

in bright lights and hold
each other captive
in fragile chains.

There's a good dance
whenever you lie still
with me and for me.
It's the best time
for singing on key
of sorrow and of wordless joy.

The Bed

When I was much younger
much more solemn than now
and couldn't watch a leaf fall
without an archetypal twitch
and every apple was original sin,
and we were new to each other,
still shy and guarded, I
wrote a poem about waking up
after the wrestle of love
and then a lonely sleep.
I wrote about the first light,
about the breathless moment when
one discovers one and one
make two. For better or worse
there would always be the two
of us to share one bed.

I can't recall it now.
I think that I compared
us to fallen angels.
And then that fancy simile
dissolved and doubled and
love was an old-fashioned dogfight
from the First World War
and lovers were Spads and Fokkers
looping, spinning, falling
in crazy trails of smoke and flame.
Then it became a shipwreck
and the world a forlorn beach
where, half-drowned, we raised
our heads to find each other
still alive and kicking.
I believe we were disappointed,

in the silly poem at least,
discovering that even in survival
being alone was a luxury.
I know how foolish it is

to try to make a drama of
a good and simple thing.
Still, it does take a while
to lose oneself enough
to measure one's delight
by another's mystery.
What a waste of time
to wait so long to learn
that love is purely a dance!
All that I wrestled with
in darkness and in light
was not angels, but myself.

Now after love we fall
easy in each other's arms.
Now sleeping is to float
on calm and moonstruck seas.
Now when I sleep I dream
of gardens where the apples are
simply beautiful. I pick one
and I offer it to you.
It's sweet and good to eat.
Now when I wake I smile
for joy to find you there.
One bed is surely plot enough
to ground our several ghosts.
And there is ample space for two
to ride the liferaft home
from shipwreck into harbor.

Belly Dance

Once I told you how
(I heard it from somebody
who swore that it was true)
the belly dance began
in ancient Egypt to instruct.
An *exemplum* for innocent brides.
It was regularly performed
at wedding parties and
given most serious attention.
I argued then (the sophist of
half a fifth of bourbon)
that it was the right thing:
proper that such knowledge
should be passed on,
decorous that it had to be,
typical of our times that nowadays
the belly dancer has to live
in the brittle scrimmy world
of nightclubs, of misplaced
erotic daydreams, of sex
in a strange greenhouse growing wild.
Where the talk went from there
I don't remember, only that,
as usual, my tongue wagged
like a lazy semaphore until
somebody else wedged in a word.
Talk will be the death of us all
yet. But, anyway, imagine
my astonishment to find you now
alone in our bedroom dancing
in front of the mirror.
You have folded your nightgown
down from the top. Your breasts
are bare and free and fine.
You have folded your nightgown
(an aquamarine and gauzy thing

I have always been amused by)
below the eye of your navel
and, from where I am standing
behind you, unseen,
in a neat line across the twin curves
of your hips. What a joy
to my eyes, first and last,
is the shape of this woman
naked! I love you,
but what in the world are you *doing?*
Arms overhead, a kind
of standing odalisque, you are
swinging hips to left and right,
a pure delight in awkward motion.
A twentieth century woman
tentatively tries an ancient dance.
Now is the time for words
and I am tonguetied. I rejoice
and laugh at the same time.
Then I step into the mirror
and you blush and are angry
because I am laughing at you.
We are a long way from Egypt now,
my love. No palms, no pyramids,
no weeping crocodiles to give
the setting for performance.
I only want you as you are,
my belly dancer. Take me
with a skeptical grain of salt.
Believe nothing except this:
As the round world moves, the moon,
the tides, so you. Like them
you are the subtle rhythms
my blood dances to. My heart
sings (wordless) to your tunes.
Let idle talk be damned!

I like the way you move
without a spotlight or snaredrum
or historical precedent.
I take you in my arms for good.
Why be so proud and lonely?
I know a dance for two.

Never Mind the Sestet. Eight Lines Are a Gracious Plenty.

for David Slavitt and his "Octaves"

You are quite right, of course, the space,
though modest, is surely ample enough to stage,
say, a play for children with one authentic witch,
a charming lazy princess and her vain stepmother,
a decent old king, befuddled by modern business management,
and his shrewd chief minister burning alive with ambition,
with still room left over for the furious prince to arrive
safely and confound us all with a simple statement.

The big bad abstractions are back in town again.
Tall, slope-bellied, shaded by wide-brimmed hats,
dragging their huge shadows by the heels, they swagger
down the empty street. A hound dog rises from his snooze
near the swinging doors of the Red Eye Saloon and slinks away
without even pausing to stretch, boneless as poured water.
Chink-a-chinka-chink, bright spurs warn a dusty world.
Beneath an enormous sombrero, a Mexican crosses himself,
and then continues to snore more loudly than before.
Acting more on inspiration than logic,
the Sheriff pins his tin star on the Town Drunk
and runs to catch the last stagecoach for California.

Meanwhile into a sunny plaza ghostly with fountains
here come the generalizations in full dress uniforms,
all lavish in polished leather and brass buttons, tilting,
nearly topheavy with medals, these brilliant officers
of the old regime. *Oompah-oompah-oompah* blares a band
while the crowds wolf down bananas and chocolate bars,
buy every balloon and pound palms raw with sweaty applause.

Now cut directly to the inevitable moment
when the smoke is finally clearing away and there they are,
heels up and spurs down, those generalizations,
hanging conventionally from the streetlamps and phone poles.
Their rows of medals make a tinkly music.
See also, flat as oriental rugs along the street,
those are abstractions who once were fast on the draw.
While buzzards circle like homesick punctuation marks,
the simple and specific common nouns come forth again
to clean up the mess and mark the spot for scholars
        (*oh oompah-oompah, chinka-chink*)
with a row of gravestones grinning like false teeth.

Tea with Expatriates

In the Villa Aurelia so many dishes

come with a cup of tea
that I might as well be a juggler
as to try to drink it and at the same time
keep track of the cookies and sandwiches,
O what a confusion of china and little spoons
is civilization trying to be at ease
    with itself!

Through the tall windows I can see
the sprawl of Rome below, the old stones
extravagantly soaking up the afternoon light.

My host complains the convent that's nearby
wakes him at six with morning hymns.
Hostess says that plumbing is a problem
and that our Embassy is grossly overstaffed.
Butler, in a white coat and pink
from a fresh shave, moves on the soft feet
    of a stalking cat.

Two French poodles, like a pair of toys,
gambol on the lawn of carpet.
There are no children in this house.

The city still glows below in slowly fading light.

Much as I am pleased
I haven't dropped or spilled
or broken anything yet
I have a powerful itch to go.

I want to go down into that last light.
To drink it, splash in it, bathe in it.
I want to be deaf in the noise of it,
the shrill and always ringing,
laughing, cursing, crying, singing
chaos of this city whose inhabitants go forth

and multiply like loaves and fishes.

Waiting alone with a hangover in the Howard Johnson Motel
I could as well be in Denver or Miami or Emporia
and could as well be (I like to think) a traveling
    salesman at least
or maybe a conventioneer, a straggler from some conference
on, let's say, new procedures and guidelines in
    modern corporate accounting.
But I am not, I cannot be; I was here, wherever I am,
to read poems and to talk about poetry with students
and my head is a booming buzzing ache of words,
words, words, my own and other people's, said and unsaid.
We wear the order of the laminated cliché like a convention badge.
    Lordy   Lordy   Lordy

Waking with a terrible hangover in Howard Johnson's,
head a hive, bowels a kennel, legs spaghetti,
eyes a tattered sunset, hands as broken wings, face
    a full moon in daylight, lonesome and irreparable,
I stagger with the heavy shame of my lazy tongue
which, before it became this thing of leather and fur,
was lively and sleek as a pair of semaphore flags.
Message as follows: I have left undone those things which I
    ought to have done *etc. etc.*
And there is no health in me.
And there is no reply.
    Lordy   Lordy   Lordy

It is always worse than I remembered, worse than I imagined.
I have worn out my welcome of words like a limp deck of cards.
The last pale one-eyed Jack, a common prankster,
relinquishes the kingdom of the blind man with one wink.
Kings and queens glare like grandparents. The Joker rings
    hateful bells in my ears.
All the aces have shaken off the dust of my shabby sleeves.
Only, inside coat pocket, the coat hanging loose on a chair,
directly in front of the mirror that I carefully avoid greeting,
inside that coat's pocket, clean in a crisp and windowed
    envelope,

the printed check waits patiently for me, virginal and wise.
Ah, money be light and music and vintage wine,
finally sweeter and stronger than the kisses of beautiful strangers,
I have cheated no one but myself. I have stolen nothing
      of real value.
For this sweet charity I'm pleased to sing like a crow or a bullfrog.
    Lordy   Lordy   Lordy

Reduced now to debit and credit, I rise from a rumpled bed
in the almost certain hope that a shower and a shave and a clean shirt,
the sweet taste of toothpaste on my tongue and teeth, will
      charm
and distract the prophet into ignoring
      the motionless mountain
and in the faith that this first swallow of whiskey in a plastic cup
will drive all my ghosts to ground and welcome again some
    charming guests.
I shall be cured of every symptom of doubt and dejection.
I shall decide that my Howard Johnson room is only cheerful.
And I shall be only cheerful in Denver, Emporia, Miami.
Ready and able to shuffle the old deck and deal under the table.
Willing to flash the latest clichés like expensive cufflinks.
Rich now in my coat of many colors, the reassuring check fitting
    comfortable and heavy like a gun in a holster,
I raise my glass to share a toast with the stranger in the mirror,
to rejoice together in the inexhaustible resources of self-deception,
beyond the deepest dreams of decent salesmen and cost accountants.
See how my hands are steady. Now I know how it is to live forever.

Little poem, the two of us know too much.
You and I can never be quite the same again.

I pretend I am gray from worrying over you
while you profess to be concerned about my health.

Walking along together, father and frisky daughter,
holding hands, we are ready to greet friends or enemies.

And I grin, thinking to myself: *You little bitch.*
Nobody else can ever love you and I couldn't care less.

But you know better: *The old man will eat his heart out,*
ravenous for the love and kisses of strangers.

Cracking and fading like an old photograph,
I am pleased to bequeath the same fate to you.

All supple and shiny now, my son,
you picture my skull and bones on a stone.

You know what happens on the dusty playgrounds,
the raw taste of knuckles, the colors of a bruise.

I know about steppes and tundra of blank paper
and stinking jungles where the words crawl like snakes.

Both of us hear voices and believe whatever they say.
In dreams we meet monsters and hold them like lovers.

We shall never talk to each other about any of this.
In all due time I hope to forget your proper name.

Grip tight, little one. Hold your head high.
Strut, you bastard, and smile at the people.

Wonderful Pen

(A Snapshot)

When I bought this wonderful pen this morning,
at Ulrich's on South University in Ann Arbor,
the lady escorted me personally to the checkout counter,
maybe because I might try to sneak out without paying
but also because it was clearly a kind of an occasion
for me and for her and (I guess) for the store.
After all, how often does someone just walk in here
and ask for and pay cash for a $185 fountain pen?

The lady tells the girl at the cash register
what the pen costs and that I get a faculty discount
of 10%. Casually, then, I peel off and plunk down
four $50 bills, poor old U. S. Grant on the front of each.
It is payday, and I am feeling good, feeling fine.
I have been saving a long time for this stubby black Mont
    Blanc
with its bright gold nib which is sure to teach me some
    golden words.
I smile. Girl glares back her altogether savage disapproval.
"Jesus Christ!" she exclaims. "People are starving in
    places like Bangladesh!
They are killing each other with clubs in Uganda and
    Cambodia!
And you—I can't fucking *believe* it!—are spending a
    fortune
on a fountain pen! What can you possibly *do* with a pen
    like that?"
Saddened, embarrassed, but refusing to feel guilty, what
    can I say?
"Lady, this pen takes moving pictures; it records human
    voices and
if you stick it up your ass, you'll suddenly find that you
    can sing
more sweet songs than a canary or a Georgia
    mockingbird."

Deep Lent and the ratty tag end
of the woodpile has dwindled now
to chips and bark   knots and elbows

Mud and muddy ice   Fog and mizzling sky
Winter is the old world's hacking cough
Birds fight for seeds in my feeder

Not smoke nor any sap is rising yet
Nor anything here can lightly dispel
the weight of this weather within me

Raw and rowdy some reedy jays
trouble the grackles and sparrows
Amazing in bare branches a cardinal

waits his turn   And so do I
O lead me not into nor leave me be
I who can scold too well enough but never

forgive myself   My boots suck mud
where I stoop and take up rotten wood
to build and burn my latest text of fire

Lord your turn comes next   All alone
on a glistening branch of pain you weep
to see us snarling over these last seeds